Frederic Pincott, Francis Johnson

Hitopadesa

A New Literal Translation from the Sanskrit Text of prof. F. Johnson

Frederic Pincott, Francis Johnson

Hitopadesa

A New Literal Translation from the Sanskrit Text of prof. F. Johnson

ISBN/EAN: 9783337188467

Printed in Europe, USA, Canada, Australia, Japan

Cover: Foto ©Thomas Meinert / pixelio.de

More available books at **www.hansebooks.com**

HITOPADESA.

A NEW

LITERAL TRANSLATION FROM THE SANSKRIT TEXT

OF PROF. F. JOHNSON.

FOR THE USE OF STUDENTS.

BY

FREDERIC PINCOTT, F.R.A.S.

LONDON:
W. H. ALLEN AND CO., 13, WATERLOO PLACE. S.W.
PUBLISHERS TO THE INDIA OFFICE.

1880.

PREFACE.

THE object of the present translation is to supply an exact and literal rendering of Professor F. Johnson's text of the Hitopades'a for the use of students learning Sanskrit. The Hitopades'a being generally the first book taken up by learners, it is obviously of importance to translate it in such a manner that one completely ignorant of Sanskrit may be guided in his first efforts. The following translation, therefore, is made somewhat progressive. The first chapter endeavours punctually to render the original,—case, tense, and even the order of the words,—as far as may be; for the purpose of showing the student how the English meaning is got out of the Sanskrit text. In the second chapter a little more ease is permitted; and in the third and fourth chapters, while still being precise and literal, the English language is allowed somewhat fairer play.

With respect to authorities, I have, of course, had before me what Sir Charles Wilkins, and Professors Johnson and Max Müller have so excellently done; but I have also enjoyed an advantage not hitherto brought to bear on the subject. Familiarity with certain of the vernaculars of India has enabled me to take the opinion of native scholars, who, so to speak, inherit the meaning of the original in the traditions and circumstances of daily life. I have, accordingly, consulted throughout a faithful translation in the Gwâlerarî dialect (India Office

MS. No. 2385), also a Hindî version, one in Bangâlî, and another in Braj Bhâkhâ. A manuscript version in Urdû, in my own possession, has been of singular assistance throughout, by frequently supplying Semitic equivalents for the Aryan words of the original. This MS. deserves editing, for it differs markedly from most native translations, inasmuch as it is a precise line for line rendering of the original, without amplification or curtailment. It is also remarkable to find a Muhammadan spend so much labour on anything Hindû.

The five translations thus availed of, were made in different provinces, at different times, by different men, probably, nay almost certainly, in profound ignorance of each other's performances. Therefore, whenever I have found five native scholars, unknown to each other, unite in ascribing a given sense to a given passage, I have felt constrained to yield some deference to their opinion.

The main point aimed at throughout has been accuracy. Fluency and elegance have been disregarded, from the assurance that any English person, with the precise rendering here supplied, can clothe the sentences in such Shakesperian or Johnsonian phraseology as his taste may suggest.

FREDERIC PINCOTT.

INTRODUCTION.

1. May there be success, for the good, in what is to be accomplished, through the favour of that Dhûrjati,* on whose brow (there is) a digit of the Moon, like a streak of foam of the Jâhnavî.†

2. This Hitopadeśa,‡ attended to, gives skill in Sanskrit speaking, variety of expression universally, and the knowledge of policy.

3. A wise man should think of knowledge and wealth as though (he were) undecaying and immortal; he should practise virtue as though seized in the hairs of the head by Death.

4. Among all things knowledge, they say, (is) truly the best thing; from, at all times, its unstealableness, its unpurchaseableness, and its indestructibility.

5. Knowledge truly unites a man with a king difficult of access, as a descending river (unites with) the ocean; hence (results) exceeding prosperity.

6. Knowledge gives prudence, from prudence one attains fitness (for work), from fitness one attains wealth, from wealth the (power of) doing good; thence (arises) happiness.

7. Arms and literature (are) both (kinds of) knowledge, (they are) the two (kinds of) knowledge (conducive) to celebrity; the first (leads) to ridicule in old age, the second is honoured always.

8. Since the pattern impressed on a new (earthern) vessel cannot become otherwise (than it is at the time of manufacture), therefore, by the artifice of fables, the moral guidance of youths is here set forth.

9. The Acquisition of Friends, the Separation of Friends, War, and Peace,—having been abstracted from the Panchatantra and another book,—is written (here).

There is on the banks of the Bhâgîrathî† a city named Pâtaliputra§: a king named Handsome, possessed of every lordly virtue, was there. This king once heard these two verses being recited by somebody:—

10. The resolver of many doubts, the revealer of invisible objects, the eye of all (is) learning; of whom it is not, he truly (is) blind.

---

* The god Siva. † The river Ganges. ‡ Meaning "friendly advice."
§ The present Patna.

1

11. Youth, riches, power, and inconsiderateness, each singly (lead) to disadvantage; how much more (so) where all four (are united)!

Having heard this, the king, distressed in mind by the inattention to books of his own sons, unread in literature, (and) ever following improper courses, reflected :—

12. What advantage accrues by a son born who (is) neither wise nor virtuous? what, by a sightless eye? Truly (such) an eye (is) trouble merely.

13. Of unborn, dead, (or) foolish (sons), better the two first, and not the last; the two first cause pain once, the last day by day.

Further :—

14. He (is really) born by whom (when) born the family attains exaltation; in the revolving world,* who, (when) dead, is not born (again)?

Besides :—

15. If a mother (be accounted) the mother of a son by (reason of) him whose chalk does not fall quickly in beginning the enumeration of a number of the virtuous, say, what (woman) is barren?

Also :—

16. He whose mind (is) not intent on liberality, sanctity, heroism, learning, and the acquisition of wealth, truly he (is his) mother's excrement.

Furthermore :—

17. Better one accomplished son: not even by a hundred fools (is there advantage); one Moon dispels darkness; (it is) not (dispelled) by even hosts of stars.

18. The son of him by whom, in some holy place, a very arduous penance has been performed, should be obedient, wealthy, virtuous, (and) wise.

And it has been said :—

19. The influx of wealth, continual healthfulness, a beloved (wife), a sweet-speaking wife, an obedient son, and profitable knowledge, (are) the six felicities of life, O king!

20. Who (is) fortunate by (the possession of) many sons, (no better than empty) measures filling the granary; better one family-supporter, by whom the father is renowned.

21. A debt-contracting father (is) an enemy, and (so is) an unchaste mother; a beautiful wife (is) an enemy, an unlearned son (is) an enemy.

22. In the absence of practice, knowledge (is) poison; in (a state of) indigestion, food (is) poison; the (royal) court (is) the poison of the poor; a young wife (is) the poison of an old (man).

23. Of whomsoever the son is gifted, (that) man is honoured; what will a bow effect, faultless (as to) cane, (but) stringless?

24. Alas, O son! (who hast) without study passed these nights! In consequence thou sinkest in the midst of the wise, like a cow in a quag-mire.

---

* The revolving series of births and deaths.

Then how can these my sons be rendered accomplished?

25. Food, sleep, fear, and sexual intercourse, this (set is) the common property of men with beasts. Virtue is their great distinction. Deprived of virtue (men are) equal with brutes.

For :—

26. He of whom there is not one of (the attributes) virtue, wealth, pleasure, (or) liberation (from transmigration), his birth (is) worthless like (that) of the pimples on a goat's neck.

And (as to) what is said:—

27. Life, (destined) acts, wealth, knowledge, and death, these five are created for a corporeal being (while in) the embryo state.

Again :—

28. There are states of what is to be inevitably even of the great, (to wit) the nakedness of Nîlakaṇṭha* (and) the sleep of Hari on the great serpent.†

And also :—

29. What is not to be will not be; if (it is) to be, it (will) not (be) otherwise (than as is foreordained). Why is not this anxiety-destroying medicine drunk?

This (is) the speech, arising from idleness, of certain persons incapable of what should be done.

30. Having thought even upon fate, one should not abandon one's own exertion; without exertion one cannot obtain oil from (even) sessamum seeds.

Besides :—

31. Prosperity attends upon the energetic lion of a man. Abject fellows say, "It is given by fate." Having resisted fate act (with) manliness with (all) thy strength. If, on effort being made, (the deed) is not accomplished, what fault (is) there?

32. Just as with one wheel there can be no motion of a chariot, so without the act of man destiny (itself) is not accomplished.

Also :—

33. An act done in a former birth is called "Fate"; therefore, unwearied, one should manfully make effort.

34. As from a lump of clay a workman produces whatever he wishes, so a man obtains the destiny prepared by himself.

Besides :—

35. Though perceiving a treasure in front, obtained like the fruit of the palm [which unexpectedly fell and revealed its rich contents to] the crow,‡ Fate itself does not pick it (up), it waits for man.

36. Deeds are accomplished by effort not by wishes; verily deer do not enter into the mouth of a sleeping lion.

37. A child trained by mother and father attains eminence; a son does not become wise by being merely born.

---

* The god Siva.   † The god Vishnu.   ‡ Alluding to a fable.

So also:—

38. The mother (is) an enemy, the father (is) a foe, by whom a child is not instructed; he [the child] shines not in company, (he is) like a heron amongst crows.

39. Possessed of beauty (and) youth, born of noble family, (but) destitute of knowledge, they shine not. (They are) like scentless kiṁśuka flowers.

40. Even a fool shines in an assembly just as (he may be) dressed; thus-long a fool shines, so long as he says nothing.

Having reflected thus the king convoked an assembly of the learned. The king (then) said: O Paṇḍits, listen. Is there any one so learned who (is) able now, by instruction in politic science, to effect the regeneration of my continually wayward and ignorant sons?

For:—
41. Glass by association with gold acquires an emerald lustre; so, by proximity to the good, a fool attains cleverness.

And it is said:—
42. The mind is indeed lowered, O son, from associated with the low; with equals it reaches equality; but with the distinguished (it attains) distinction.

Hereupon a great scholar named Vishṇuśarman, like Vrihaspati, conversant with the gist of all books on policy, said: Sire! these princes born in a high family can be caused to acquire policy by me. For:—

43. No labour whatever bestowed on a worthless object can be fruitful: even by a hundred efforts a crow is not made to talk like a parrot.

Moreover:—
44. But in this family worthless offspring is not born: In a mine of rubies whence (can arise) the production of crystal?

Hence I, in the period of six months, will make your sons conversant with works of policy. The king courteously replied:—

45. Even a worm by association with a jasmine ascends (above) the head of the good: even a stone attains divinity, (when) consecrated by the great.

Besides:—
46. As, upon the eastern mountain an object shines by the drawing near (of the sun), so by the proximity of the good even an out-caste is enlightened.

47. The virtuous are discriminators of right and wrong; should they acquire vice they become faulty: rivers arise (having their) waters sweet; having reached the ocean they become undrinkable.

Therefore you (are) the authority for the instruction in politic science of these my sons. Having said thus, with much courtesy he consigned his sons to Vishṇuśarman Then, in the presence of the princes, comfortably seated on the terrace of the palace, by way of introduction, the Paṇḍit said : O princes, listen—

48. With the enjoyment of poetic works the time of the wise passes, and (that) of fools with vice, sleep, or contention.

Therefore, for the gratification of your Highnesses, I (am about to) relate the wonderful story of the crow, the tortoise, &c. The princes said: Sir, let it be related. Vishṇuśarman said: Listen now; the "Acquisition of Friends" is commencing, of which this (is) the first verse:—

ACQUISITION OF FRIENDS.

1. The wise and very friendly Crow, Tortoise, Deer, and Mouse, without means, (and) destitute of wealth, speedily accomplished (their) purposes.

The princes said : How is that? Vishṇuśarman relates (as follows):—There is on the bank of the Godâvarî* a large silk-cotton tree; there, having assembled from various quarters and countries, birds at night are roosting. Now on a certain night being ended, when the revered Moon, the friend of the lotus (was) resting on the summit of the western mountain, a crow, named Gently-alighting, being awake, saw a fowler approaching snare in hand like a second Death. Having seen him, he reflected (thus): To-day, even betimes, an unwished for sight has appeared. I do not know what undesired (circumstance) it will reveal. So saying, following him gradually, he moved perplexed.

For :—

2. Thousands of occasions of grief, and hundreds of occasions of fear, day by day approach the fool, not the wise.

Moreover :—

By worldlings this indispensably should be done:—

3. Each day one rises, it should be thought, a great danger is imminent; of death, sickness, or sorrow, which will happen to-day?

Now having scattered grains of rice, a net was spread by the fowler, and he being concealed remained (waiting). Just at that time, the king of the pigeons, named Speckled-neck, gliding in the sky with (his) retinue, saw those grains of rice. Then the king of the pigeons, perceiving the pigeons covetous of the grains of rice, remarked : Whence (comes) the origin of grains of rice here in (this) deserted wood ? Let this be investigated a little. I do not look upon this (as) fortunate. Haply by this covetousness for grains of rice, we also in like manner may become—

4. As the traveller, sunk in an impassable quag-mire, seized by an old tiger, perished, through covetousness of a bracelet.

---

* In the Dakkhan.

The pigeons said: How (was) that? The king of the pigeons relates (as follows): Once, while feeding in the Southern forest, I observed an old tiger, (who had) bathed, with kuśa-grass in (his) paw, on the banks of a lake, was saying: Ho, ho, traveller, let this golden bracelet be accepted. Then, attracted by avarice, a certain traveller (thus) reflected: This arises by good luck;—but in this (enterprize entailing) risk within itself an attempt is not to be made.

For:—

5. In the acquisition of the desired from the undesired, a felicitous result does not arise; where there is the presence of poison, there even ambrosia (tends) to death.

But everywhere in the acquisition of wealth, the attempt (is) a risk. Thus it has been said:—

6. Not having surmounted doubt a man sees not good things; on the contrary, having overcome doubt, if he lives, he sees (them).

Therefore, I (will) investigate a little. He says aloud, Where (is) thy bracelet? The tiger having stretched forth (his) paw shows (it). The traveller said: How (is) confidence to be placed in thee, a ferocious (animal)? The tiger said: Listen, traveller-fellow! formerly, of a truth, in a youthful state, I was excessively wicked. Through the slaughter of many cows, Brâhmans, and men, my numerous children are dead, and (my) wife (also). Now I am without family. Therefore, by a certain virtuous (person) I was advised (thus): Let your honour practise the duty of liberality. In consequence of his advice now I (am) a practiser of ablutions, a bestower (of alms), old, (and) with decayed claws and teeth; how (am I) not a (fit) object of confidence.

It is said:—

7. Sacrifice, study, alms-giving, self-mortification, truth, fortitude, patience, and contentment,—this, it is said, (is) the eight-fold path of duty.

8. The former four-fold class is practised in this world even for ostentation; but the latter four-fold class dwells only in the magnanimous.

And my freedom from cupidity (is) such that the golden bracelet belonging even to my own arm, I am willing to give to anyone soever. Still (it is) really hard to remove the common imputation to the effect that tigers eat men. For:—

9. The world, following precedent, does not constitute a good-counselling bawd an authority in virtue, as (it does) even cow-killing Brâhman.

And by me religious books have been studied. Listen:—

10. As rain on a desert place so (is) food (bestowed) on one pained by hunger. A fruitful gift is (one) bestowed on the poor, O son of Pâṇḍu!

11. As one's own vital airs [life] are cherished, so also (should be) those of (other) creatures. By reason of self-likeness* the good exercise compassion on (other) beings.

Besides:—

12. Both in refusing, and in bestowing, in pleasure and pain, in the agreeable and in the disagreeable, by self-likeness a man attains a (good) authority.

---

* Referring all things to self as a standard.

MITRALÂBHÂ.   7

Again:—
13. He who looks upon another's wife as a mother, on another's wealth as a clod, on all beings as himself, he (is) wise.

And thou (art) unfortunate; therefore I (am) anxious to give to thee. And it is said:—

14. Nourish the poor, O son of Kuntî; do not give wealth to the wealthy. For the sick, medicine (is) beneficial; but what (do) the healthy (want) with medicines?

Besides:—
15. "It is to be given," thus (is the command; therefore) whatever gift is bestowed upon the non-assistant, in a (right) place, time, and on a (proper) recipient, that they esteem a virtuous gift.

Therefore, having bathed in the lake, accept this golden bracelet. Then, confiding in his speech, as soon as he had entered the lake to bathe, immediately he sank into a great quag-mire, (and) was unable to escape. Seeing him fallen into the quag-mire the tiger said: Ha! thou art fallen into a great quag-mire, therefore I (will) lift thee up. Having said thus, (and) having cautiously approached,—the traveller, seized by the tiger, reflected (thus):

16. " He reads the Dharma-śâstras," this is not the operative cause; neither (is) the repetition of the Veda. The natural disposition of the wicked truly here predominates; just as by (its) nature the milk of the cow is sweet.

Again:—
17. The act of those whose senses and heart are not under control (is) like the washing of an elephant.* Knowledge without practice (is) a burden, like ornaments on an ill-disposed wife.

Therefore it was not well done by me, that confidence was here reposed in a ferocious (animal). Thus truly is it said:—

18. Confidence should never be placed in rivers, in those with weapons in their hands, in those with claws or horns, in women, and in kings' families.

Besides:—
19. Of everyone, indeed, the natural dispositions are tested, not the other qualities; transcending all (other) qualities the natural disposition is at the head.

Moreover:—
20. Truly he, sporting in the sky, destroying darkness, possessed of ten hundred beams, moving in the midst of stars, even the Moon, by reason of destiny, is swallowed by Râhu.† Who is able to avoid what is written on the forehead?

While reflecting thus he was killed and eaten by the tiger: hence I say, " By covetousness of a bracelet," &c. Therefore a not properly considered act ought, by no means, to be done.

For:—
21. Well-digested food, a circumspect son, a well-governed wife, a well-served king, a well-considered speech, and a well-deliberated act, in a very long time undergoes no change.

---

* Unefficacious in character.   † Is subject to eclipse.

Having heard this speech a certain pigeon haughtily said: Ah! what indeed is being said?

22. On the time of adversity being imminent, the speech of the aged ought to be received everywhere, indeed, with consideration: it is not concerned in eating.

For:—

23. All food and drink is beset, on the face of the earth, with doubts: where is anything to be done? or how (is) the possibility of living?

And it is said:—

24. The envious, the censorious, the discontented, the passionate, the ever-suspicious, and he who lives on another's fortune,—these six have misery for their portion.

Having heard this, all the pigeons alighted there. For:—

25. The very learned, resolvers of doubts, versed in even the greatest sciences, (when) fascinated by covetousness are afflicted.

Again:—

26. From covetousness proceeds anger; from anger lust is produced; from covetousness (arises) both infatuation and perdition. Covetousness (is) the cause of sin.

Again:—

27. The production of a golden deer (is) an impossibility; still Râma lusted for the deer*; oft-times, at a season of impending calamity, even the intellects of the masculine become clouded.

Presently they were all caught in the net. Then all the birds abuse him through whose speech they had alighted there. Thus it is said:—

28. One should not go in front of the troop,—when the act has succeeded the profit (is) equal; should there be a disaster in the affair, the leader is killed on the spot.

And it is said:—

29. Unrestraint of the senses is said (to be) the path of misfortune; the conquest of them (is) the path of success: go by whichever (path) is desired (by you).

Hearing the abuse of him Speckled-neck said: This (is) not his fault. For:—

30. Even a friend becomes the cause of misfortunes which happen: even a mother's leg becomes a post on the binding of a calf.†

Again:—

31. He is a friend who (is) able to remove the calamity of the unfortunate; but not (he who is) skilful in censuring means for deliverance from what is apprehended.

And in time of misfortune of a truth perplexity is the sign of a coward; therefore now, resting (on) fortitude, let a remedy be thought of. For:—

32. In misfortune firmness, in prosperity meekness, in the assembly eloquence, in war valour, in fame desire, perseverance in study,—this (is) the perfection of the nature of the magnanimous.

---

* The magical appearance of a golden deer deluded him. † At the time of milking.

33. Of whom, in prosperity, (there is) no exaltation, (nor) dejection in adversity, and (who is) firm in battle,—a mother rarely gives birth to that son, the ornament of the three worlds.

Besides:—
34. Six faults should be here shunned by a man wishing for dignity,—sleep, sloth, fear, anger, laziness, (and) prolixity.

Now let it thus be done,—being of one mind, the net being taken up by the whole, let (us) fly away.

For:—
35. The combination of even little things (is) effective of what is to be done: by grasses (which have) become cord furious elephants are bound.

36. The best combination for men (is) with their own families, although small; stripped of their husks grains of rice do not germinate.

Having reflected thus, all the birds, taking up the net, started up. Hereupon the fowler from afar having seen those removers of the net, running after (them) reflected—

37. Those travellers of the air, combined, are carrying off my net; when they alight then they will come (into) my power.

Then, upon the birds passing beyond the range of sight, the fowler desisted. Now having seen (that) the fowler had desisted, the pigeons said: Sire! what now (is) proper to be done? Speckled-neck said:—

38. A mother, a friend, and a father,—from natural disposition (form) a friendly trio; and others from special cause are friendly-minded.

My friend, then, named Well-to-do, the king of the mice, dwells in Pretty-wood, on the banks of the Gaṇḍakî; he will sever our bonds by the strength of his teeth. Having decided thus, all went near to the burrow of Well-to-do. But Well-to-do, through continual apprehension of danger, having constructed a burrow with a hundred entrances, is dwelling (therein).

39. Perceiving danger not yet arrived, an old mouse, skilled in books of policy, occupied there a burrow with a hundred openings.

Then Well-to-do, startled by the descent of the pigeons, remained silent. Speckled-neck said: O friend Well-to-do, why art thou not conversing (with) us? Well-to-do having heard his observation (and) recognised (him), ran out hastily (and) said: Ah! I am fortunate, my dear friend Speckled-neck (is) come!

40. Who has converse with a friend, who has (his) abode with a friend, who has condolence with a friend,—there is none here more fortunate than he!

Seeing them bound in a snare, remaining a moment with amazement, he said: O friend! what (is) this? Speckled-neck replied: This (is) the result of our conduct in a former birth.

41. From whomsoever, and by whomsoever, and howsoever, and whensoever, and whatsoever, and how much soever, and wheresoever—good and evil (there may happen to be, it is) one's own act, and comes from the predominance of Fate.

42. Sickness, sorrow, regret, bonds, and afflictions,—these (are) the fruits of the tree of the personal offences of corporeal beings.

Hearing this Well-to-do hastily drew near to sever the bonds of Speckled-neck. Thereupon Speckled-neck says: O friend, by no means so; first just sever the snare of these my dependants. Well-to-do replied: I (am) weak, and my teeth are soft; then how am I able to cut the noose of these many? Therefore, as long as my teeth do not break so long (will) I cut thy noose; after that, to the utmost of my power, I will sever the bonds of the others also. Speckled-neck said: Be it even so; still to the utmost of thy power break the bonds of these. Well-to-do replied: The preservation of followers by the abandonment of self (is) not approved by those who are conversant with policy.

For :—

43. (A man) should preserve his wealth on account of misfortune, with his wealth also he should preserve (his) wife; both by wealth (and) by wife he should always preserve himself.

Again :—

44. The vital airs (are) the causes of the continuance of virtue, wealth, pleasure, and (final) deliverance; by destroying these [vital airs] what (is) not destroyed, by preserving (them) what (is) not preserved?

Speckled-neck said: O friend, policy, truly, (is) just such as this; but I am not able to endure the affliction of my dependants; therefore, I say this. For :—

45. A wise man would relinquish riches and even life on account of another: death being certain, better the abandonment (of life) in a good cause.

And this (is) another especial reason :—

46. Among these, there is community of race, wealth, and qualities with me; state (then) the advantage of my sovereignty; when and what will that be?

Besides :—

47. Of a truth, these without recompense do not quit my vicinity; therefore, even at the expense of my life preserve these my dependants.

Again :—

48. Abandoning solicitude on (account of) this perishable body, formed of flesh, urine, excrement, and bone, preserve my reputation, O friend!

And see further :—

49. If eternal unsullied fame can be obtained by the transitory body charged with impurities, why, then, should (it) not be obtained?

For :—

50. Between the body and the virtues (there is) an exceedingly wide difference; the body (is) perishable in an instant, the virtues endure to the end of time.

Hearing this, Well-to-do, being delighted in mind (and) having the hairs of the body erect (with pleasure), replied: Good, O friend, good! by this tenderness for thy dependants the sovereignty of even the three worlds is suited to thee. Having said so, the bonds of all the pigeons (are) cut (by him). Then Well-to-do, having courteously congratulated all (of them), replied: Friend Speckled-neck, here the binding in the net being altogether fate, disparagement is not to be cast on thyself (from) suspecting a fault.

For :—

51. The bird who from more than a hundred leagues sees here the prey, even he at the appointed time, sees not the thong of the noose.

And also :—

52. The Râhu-paining of both Moon and Sun, also the binding of both elephant and snake, and the poverty of the intelligent,—having seen (all these), "O fate (is) powerful," this (is) my opinion.

Again :—

53. Even birds, solitary wanderers in the air, meet with misfortune; also fish are caught by the skilful from the sea (whose) waters (are) unfathomable. On fate (being) really unpropitious, whence (comes benefit from) good conduct? what advantage (is there) in obtaining a position? Truly Time, with hand stretched out for destruction, seizes even from afar.

Having thus counselled, exercised hospitality, and embraced, Speckled-neck, dismissed by him, with (his) retinue went to the place (he) desired.

54. Whoever (they may be) friends should be made, and hundreds (of them): behold, by the friendship of a mouse the pigeons are released from bonds.

Well-to-do, also, entered his burrow. Now the crow named Gently-alighting, a spectator of the whole occurrence, with astonishment said this: O, Well-to-do! thou art to be be praised: therefore I also desire to form friendship with thee, hence thou shouldst favour me with (thy) friendship. Hearing that, Well-to-do, remaining in the interior of his burrow, said: Who (art) thou, Sir? The crow replied: I am the crow called Gently-alighting. Then Well-to-do laughing said: What friendship (can there be) with thee?

For :—

55. What, with whatever is concordant in the world, that the wise should associate therewith: I (am) the food, you (are) the cater; how shall there be friendship (between us)?

56. Friendship between the food and the cater, (is) assuredly the cause of misfortune. The deer caught in a noose through a jackal was rescued by a crow.

The crow asked: How (was) that? Well-to-do relates (as follows) :—

There is in the country of Magadha* a forest called Champakavatî; in it for a long time, with great friendship, a deer and a crow dwelt; and the deer, delighted and plump, roaming about by its own inclination, was seen by a certain jackal. Having seen him, the jackal reflected (thus): Ah! how (may) I devour this delicate flesh of the deer? Be it as it may, I (will) just excite (his) confidence. Having reflected thus

---

* The modern Bihâr.

(and) drawn near, he said: Friend! prosperity to thee! Quoth the deer: Who (art) thou? The jackal replied: I am the jackal named Little-sense; here in the forest, destitute of friend and relation, like one dead, I am dwelling alone; but now having met with you (as a) friend, I have again entered the land of the living; now by all means, let me become a dependant of thine. The deer said: Let it be so. Afterwards, as soon as the glorious (sun) wreathed in scorching rays, had reached the western mountain, the deer and the jackal went towards the dwelling-place of the deer. There, upon the branch of a Champaka-tree, the crow named Intelligent, long the friend of the deer, was dwelling. Seeing those two, the crow exclaimed: O friend deer! who (is) this second (person)? The deer replied: This (is) a jackal come seeking my friendship. Says the crow: Friend, confidence, all of a sudden, with a new-comer is not, indeed, proper. That (is) not propitious behaviour.

Thus it is said:
57. Of whomsoever the race and disposition are unknown, (to him) house-room should not be given. Through the fault of a cat, the vulture Old-ox was killed.

They both asked: How (was) that? The crow relates:

There is on the banks of the Bhâgîrathî,* on a mountain called Vulture-peak, a large waved-leaf fig-tree. In a hollow of it, by the cruelty of fate (with) decayed claws and eyes, an old vulture named Old-ox is dwelling. Now compassionately, for his support, the birds dwelling in that tree give (him) each a little from his own food: with that he lives. Now, once upon a time, a cat named Long-ear came there to devour the young birds. Then, having seen him approaching, the young birds agitated by fear made an uproar. Hearing that, Old-ox said: Who (is) this coming? Long-ea_ perceiving the vulture timidly said: Ah! I am killed!

For:—
58. As long as danger is not imminent, so long (is) the fear of danger to be entertained; but having perceived danger at hand a man should act becomingly.

Now from extreme nearness flight is impossible, therefore as it is to be, so let it be; I (will) go near him. Having resolved thus (and) approached, he said: Sir, I salute thee. The vulture cried out: Who art thou? He replied: (It is) I, a cat. Says the vulture: Ah, miscreant! go away to a distance, otherwise thou wilt be killed by me. The cat (then) said: Just let my speech be heard, afterwards if I deserve death, then let (me) be killed.

For:—
59. Whoever is, anywhere, killed or honoured merely on account of birth? having scrutinized the conduct, he should be either killed or honoured.

Says the vulture: Tell me, of what sort (is thy) conduct? He replied: Here I am dwelling on the bank of the Ganges, continually performing ablutions, eating

---

* The river Ganges.

no flesh, as a religious student practising the Chândrâyaṇa vow.* The birds, the objects of the love and confidence of you (who are) conversant with the law, are for ever before me praising thy manifold virtues, hence I am come here to listen to an exposition of the law from your Honour, advanced in knowledge and years; and (doth) your Honour so understand the law as (to be) ready to slay me, a guest? But this has been declared the duty of a householder—

60. On even an enemy arrived at the house becoming hospitality should be bestowed; the tree does not withdraw its sheltering shadow from the wood-cutter.

Moreover, if there is no food in the house, then with very kind language at least a stranger should be entertained. For it is said :—

61. Grass, a space, water, and, fourthly, courteous language,—these are never withheld in the house of the good.

Besides :—
62. If either a child, or an old man, or a youth, come to the house, respect should be shown for him. The guest is everyone's superior.

Again :—
63. The good show pity upon even worthless beings: the moon does not withdraw (its) light from the house of the Châṇḍâla.†

Further :—
64. From whose house a guest turns away disappointed, he [the guest] goes having given to him [the householder] his (own) misdeeds, and having taken away his [the householder's] virtue.

Moreover :—
65. Even a low person come to the house of one of even the highest caste should be suitably entertained : a guest consists of all the deities.‡

The vulture replied : since cats are delighters in flesh and young birds live here, therefore I speak thus. On hearing this the cat having touched the earth, touches both (her) ears, and says: By me, with extinguished passions, studying the books of the law, this very arduous task, the Chândrâyaṇa, has been undertaken. For of the mutually discordant works of sacred authority (there is) unanimity on this point, that inoffensiveness (is) a paramount duty.

For :—
66. The men who abstain from injury to all, who patiently endure all, and who (are) the asylum of all, those men go to heaven.

Again :—
67. Virtue (is) truly the one friend which follows after (its possessor) even in death ; but all else attains equal destruction with the body.

Moreover :—
68. When anyone eats the flesh of another, behold ye the difference of the two : of the one (there is) momentary gratification, the other is abandoned by the vital airs.§

And also :—
69. The pain which is produced for a man (by the thought, "I) must die," by that reflection another (person) ought to be preserved.

---

* A fast enduring for a month.
‡ Is an impersonation of all the deities.
† A member of the lowest cast.
§ *i.e.*, is deprived of life.

Listen again :—

70. It [the stomach] is thoroughly satisfied even by vegetables spontaneously produced in the wood; on account of this craving stomach what man would commit sin?

Having thus inspired confidence the cat remained in the hollow of the tree. Then in succeeding days, attacking the young birds and bringing (them) into the hole, day by day he devours (them). Now by those disconsolate birds whose young had been devoured an investigation was commenced here and there. Perceiving that, the cat slipping out of the hole fled. Afterwards, by the birds searching hither and thither, there, in the hollow (of the tree), the bones of the young ones were found; and immediately concluding that their young ones had been eaten by him, the vulture was killed by the birds combined together. Hence I say, "Without knowing family and disposition," &c. Having heard this the jackal angrily said: On the first day of the Deer's seeing (you) your Honour also was unknown as to disposition; then how (is it that) even to the present day the course of this great affection with your Honour increases more and more?

71. Where there is not a wise person, there one of even little sense is commendable; in a country devoid of trees even the castor-oil plant ranks as a tree.

Besides :—
72. "(Is) he of my country or a stranger?" such is the calculation of the narrow-minded: the earth itself (is) the family of the noble-hearted.

And as this deer (is) my friend so (is) your Honour also. Says the deer: What (is to be effected) by this debating? let us all remain with confidential discourse enjoying happiness together. For :—

73. Noone (is) the friend of anyone, noone is the enemy of anyone; by conduct friends are produced, so (are) enemies.

The crow replied : Let it be so. Now in the early morning all went to the place they liked best. One day the jackal secretly says: In one part of this forest there is a field full of corn; having taken thee there I (will) show (it). Upon (this) being so done, the deer every day going there eats the corn. Then, in the course of a few days, having noticed him, by the owner of the field a snare was fixed there. Afterwards, the deer came again, (and) grazing there, was caught by the snare. Who, thought he, other than a friend (is) able to draw me hence from the snare of the hunter so like the noose of Death? Hereupon the jackal having approached there stood near (and) reflected : Ah! successful so far (is) our deceitful plot, the fulfilment of my wishes will also be abundant; for his flesh-and-blood stained bones on being cut up are certainly to be obtained by me. But on seeing him the deer delighted said: Friend Jackal, just sever my bonds; speedily deliver me.

For :—
74. In misfortunes one may know a friend, in battle a hero, in debt an honest person, in decaying fortunes a wife, and kinsmen in afflictions.

Moreover:—

75. He (is) a kinsman who stands (with one) in festive seasons, and also in affliction, in famine, in tumult of the country, in the king's porch, and in the cemetery.

The jackal, having inspected the snare again and again, thought (within himself): This deer is so far fast bound in the snare, and says: Friend deer, these thongs are formed of sinews, therefore how (can) I touch them with (my) teeth now on a sacred day. (My) friend! let us think (quite) otherwise. Therefore to-morrow morning whatever (shall) be suggested by thee that (will) be done by me. Having spoken thus he remained silently waiting in [the cover] of a thin bush. Meanwhile the crow, in the evening, finding the deer had not returned, searching hither and thither, having seen him in above-described condition, said: O friend, what (is) this? The deer replied: This (is) the result of despising a friend's counsel. As it has been said:

76. Misfortune (is) near him who hearkens not to the voice of well-wishing friends: that man (is) the delight of his enemies.

The crow says: Where (is) the jackal? The deer replied: Truly here he stands in the little grove waiting for my flesh. Says the crow: Friend, as much was said by me before.

77. "I have done no wrong,"—this (is) not a reason for confidence: there ever exists danger to the virtuous from the vicious.

78. One departing this life neither smells the stench of an expiring lamp, nor hears the advice of a friend, nor sees the star Arundhatî.*

79. One should avoid that kind of friend (which) behind the back injures (one's) purposes, and before the face speaks sweetly. (He is) a dish of poison with milk on the surface.

Then the crow sighing deeply (said): O wretch, what has been done by thee, agent of wickedness!

For:—

80. What (great affair) is it for those talked over with honied words, for those subdued by false services, and for hopeful and trusting suitors, to be deceived in this world!

Again:—

81. O venerable Earth! how art thou supporting that treacherous man who practises wickedness upon an unsuspecting pure-minded benefactor!

82. One should bring about neither friendship nor even acquaintance with a wicked person: charcoal (when) hot, burns; (when) cold it blackens the hand.

For this (is) the habit of wicked people,—

83. First he falls at the feet, (then) he bites the back-flesh, in the ear some charming tune or other he gently murmurs; having detected an opening he suddenly enters without fear. The mosquito practises every act of the vile.

---

* The morning star. Mythologically, the daughter of Daksha and wife of Dharma or Vas'ishṭha.

And thus—

84. A wicked person (may be) sweetly spoken, but that is not a reason for confiding (in him). He has sweetness on the tip of the tongue, (but) in the heart virulent poison.

Now early in the morning, the owner of the field, staff in hand, coming to that place, was descried by the crow. Perceiving him the crow said: Friend deer, making thyself appear like dead, filling (thy) belly with wind, (and) stiffening the legs, remain (still). When I make the sound "Caw," then hastily starting up thou wilt flee away. The deer remained just as directed by the crow. Then (he) was perceived by the owner of the field with eyes expanded with joy. Seeing the deer in the above-described condition, "Ah! this deer has died of itself," exclaiming thus, the owner of the field, having released the deer from the bond, began to fold up the snare. Then, on the owner of the field being retired a little distance, the deer hearing the noise of the crow hastily got up (and) fled away. Aiming at him, the staff was thrown by the owner of the field; (and) the jackal was killed by the blow of the staff hurled by him.

Thus it is said :—

85. Within three years, within three months, within three fortnights, within three days, one enjoys, even here, the fruit of extraordinary vices and virtues.

Hence I say, "Confidence between the food and the eater," &c. The crow replied :—

86. Even by thee (being) eaten (there would) not (be) a complete meal for me: on thee living I live, O (thou) harmless as Speckled-neck!

Again :—

87. Even among brutes, whose actions (are) pure and single, confidence (is) seen; from the excellent disposition of the good, the natural quality varies not.

Moreover :—

88. The mind of the good even (when) angered undergoes no change: the water of the ocean cannot be made hot by a wisp of straw.

Well-to-do says: Thou (art) fickle (and) friendship with the fickle should by no means be formed. Thus it is said :—

89. A cat, a buffalo, a ram, a crow, and a base man; these through confidence are ascendent, therefore confidence (in them is) inexpedient.

Furthermore you (are) on the side of our enemies; and it is said—

90. With an enemy one should not ally oneself, at least with a closely cemented union : even well heated water quenches the fire.

91. A bad person is to be avoided even although adorned with knowledge: the serpent (is) ornamented with a jewel; (but) is not he dangerous?

92. What is impossible that cannot be, what is possible that truly can be: a cart goes not on the water, a ship goes not on the land.

Besides :—
93. He who, through great affluence of wealth, confides in enemies and in an alienated wife,—that (is) the end of his life.

Gently-alighting says: All has been heard by me; still such (is) my determination that friendship with thee must absolutely be formed by me, otherwise, by my abstention from food, at thy door my body (is) to be abandoned. Thus, indeed—

94. A bad person is like an earthen vessel easy to break and difficult to repair; but a good person, like a vessel of gold, (is) hard to break and quick to be united.

Moreover :—
95. Union of all metals (is) from fluidity, of beasts and birds from instinct, of fools from fear and avarice, of good people from merit.

Moreover :—
96. Good people are seen to be formed like the cocoa-nut; others, formed like the jujube, (are) charming enough externally.

Knowing this, the society of the good is desired.

For :—
97. Even, upon an interruption of friendship, the qualities of the good undergo no change: even when broken the fibres of lotus-stalks are connected.

Besides :—
98. Purity, liberality, heroism, community of pleasures and pains, kindness, attachment, and truthfulness, (are) the qualities of a friend.

What friend other than yourself can be found by me endowed with these qualities ? Having heard this and more (of) his discourse, Well-to-do, issuing forth, said: I (am) invigorated by this nectar of your Honour's words; for it is said :—

99. Neither bathing with very cool waters, nor a pearl necklace, nor sandal-ointment although applied to every limb, so gratifies one distressed by heat, as the conversation of good people, adorned with good taste (and) resembling an attracting charm, has power for the gratification of the mind of the virtuous.

Besides :—
100. Betrayal of confidence, importunity, harshness, fickleness of mind, anger, untruthfulness, and gambling,—this (is) the spoiling of a friend.

Not even one fault, then, throughout the course of this speech, is perceptible in thee.

For :—
101. Eloquence (or) truthfulness is known by the appropriateness of the statement; unsteadiness (or) unwaveringness is ascertained by observation.

Again :—
102. The friendship of one whose heart is pure is, indeed, of one kind; the speech of one whose mind is affected by deceit acts in a quite opposite way.

103. In the mind of the wicked (there is) one thing, in the word something else, in the deed something else: in the mind of the large-souled (there is) singleness, in the word singleness, in the deed singleness.

Then let it be even as your Honour wishes; saying this Well-to-do, having established friendship, (and) having gratified the crow with choice food, entered (his) burrow. The crow also departed to his own place. After that some time passes away with their mutual presents of food, inquiries after health, and confidential conversation. One day the crow said to Well-to-do: Friend, this (is) a place (in which) the food of a crow is very hard to be procured; therefore, quitting this, I wish to go to another place. Well-to-do says:—

104. Teeth, hair, nails, (and) men, removed from their place, are not beautiful; knowing this, the wise should not abandon his own place.

The crow says: Friend, this (is) the speech of a coward.

For:—

105. Lions, good men, (and) elephants, having abandoned a place go (onwards in life); crows, cowards, (and) deer, meet death at the same spot.

Besides:—

106. What (is) recognised by an intelligent hero as his own country? or what as a foreign land? Whatever country he resorts to, even that he makes (his own), acquired by strength of arm. Whatever forest the lion ranges, striking with teeth, claws, and tail, in that same he slakes his thirst with the blood of stricken elephants.

Well-to-do asks: Whither must (we) go? For thus it is said:—

107. The wise man moves with one foot, (and) rests still with one foot: without having inspected another place, he should not abandon a former station.

The crow says: Friend, there is a well inspected place; I am (about to) lead you there. Well-to-do said: What (is) that? The crow relates: There is in the Daṇḍaka-forest a lake called Camphor-white. There, a beloved friend of mine, acquired a long time ago, the innately virtuous tortoise named Torpid, dwells. For:—

108. In advising others, wisdom may be easy for all; but in the (path of) duty the following oneself (is) for one of exalted mind.

And he will regale me with choice fish-diet. Well-to-do said: Remaining here, what is to be done by me? For:—

109. In whatever country (there is) neither respect for the good, nor the means of livelihood, nor friends, nor the advance of knowledge: anyone should abandon that country.

Besides:—

110. A rich man, a religious teacher, a king, a river, and fifthly a physician;—

where (these) five are not one should not make (one's) abode.

Again :—
111. Traffic, fear, modesty, honesty, (and) generosity,—where (those) five are not, there one should not make an abiding-place.

Again :—
112. There, O Friend, one must not dwell, where this quarternion is not—a payer of debts, a physician, a religious teacher, (and) a river of wholesome water.

Hence conduct me also there. The crow replied: Let it be so. Now the crow set out towards that pool with that friend, happy in discoursing on various subjects. Then Torpid even from afar perceiving Gently-alighting, rose up, (and) having accorded (him) a suitable welcome, performed the duties of hospitality also for the mouse. For :—

113. The preceptor of the twice-born (is) fire; a Bráhman (is) the preceptor of (other) castes; a husband (is) the sole preceptor of women : a guest (is) the preceptor everywhere.

The crow said : Friend Torpid, render especial honour to this one; for he is the chief of virtuous actors, an ocean of compassion, named Well-to-do, king of the mice. The praise of his virtue not even the Serpent-king with (his) two thousand tongues is able to celebrate. Having said this, he related the anecdote of Speckled-neck. Then Torpid, having respectfully saluted Well-to-do, said : Sir, thou shouldst state the reason of your coming to (this) desolate wood. Well-to-do replied : I am (about to) relate (it); listen. There is, in a town called Champaka, a residence for mendicants. A mendicant is dwelling there named Tufted-ear; and he goes to sleep (after) having placed on a peg (his) alms-dish, containing the food given in alms, the remains of meals; and I, having leaped up, each day used to eat this food. Afterwards his beloved friend, a mendicant named Lute-eared, arrived. Engaged with him in various topics of conversation, for the purpose of frightening me, with a piece of split cane, Tufted-ear kept striking the earth. Perceiving this, Lute-eared said : Friend, how is it that, inattentive to my conversation, you (are) intent on something else ? For :—

114. A pleased countenance, and a clear eye, attention to conversation, and sweet speech, exceeding kindness, and a ready aspect, (is) ever the mark of an attached person.

115. Giving dissatisfaction, ungratefulness, disrespect, publishing (one's) failings, the forgetting (one's) name during conversation, (is) the mark of a person of estranged nature.

Tufted-ear said : Dear Sir! I (am) not inattentive. But see, this mouse, my injurer, continually devours the alms-food remaining in the dish. Lute-eared, having examined the peg, said : How (is it that) this very weak mouse jumps so far ? therefore, here there must be some cause.

Thus it has been said :—
116. A young woman suddenly having seized the hair (and) unmercifully em-

braced, kisses (her) old husband: here there will be a cause.

Tufted-ear asks: How (is) that? Lute-eared relates (as follows): There is in Gaur a city called Kauśâmbin*; in it dwells a very wealthy merchant named Sandal-slave; and by him, when in the latter part of life, with mind overpowered by desire, through pride of wealth, was espoused a merchant's daughter named Wanton. But she was (in) the bloom of youth, like the banner of Cupid†; and an old husband was not to her satisfaction. For :—

117. The heart of those pinched by cold delights not in the moon, (nor) of those oppressed by heat in the sun, (so, the hearts) of women (take no delight) in a husband whose sensual organs are impaired by age.

Moreover :—

118. Upon the grey hairs of a man appearing, what passion forsooth (can there be)? since women, with hearts fixed on others, esteem (him) as a drug.

But the old husband was exceedingly attached (to) her. For :—

119. The hope of wealth, and the love of life (are) always important among living creatures; for an old man, a young wife is more important than life itself.

Also :—

120. A decrepit man is neither able to enjoy nor to renounce sensual objects; (as) a toothless dog only licks a bone with (his) tongue.

Now this Wanton, from the rashness of youth, overstepping family bounds, became in love with a certain merchant's son. For :—

121. Liberty, residence in a father's house, attendance at festive processions, unrestraint in the presence of tribesmen, also residence in a foreign country, the repeatedly consorting with unchaste women, the wasting away of her own means of subsistence, the old age, jealousy, (and) sojourn abroad of the husband, (are) the cause of the destruction of women.

Besides :—

122. Drinking, associating with bad people, and absence (from) the husband, roaming about, sleep, and dwelling in another's house, (are) the six faults of women.

Moreover :—

123. There is no place; there is no opportunity; there is no male a suitor;—through that, O Nârada, the chastity of women arises.

Again :—

124. Among women, no male is either agreeable or disagreeable; like cows in a forest they seek grass fresh and fresh.

125. Women, truly, (are) ever inconstant, (this is) notorious even among the celestials; lucky (are) those men of whom they (are) preserved (pure).

---

* Meaning "possessed of grass and water." † *i.e.*, was beautiful.

126. (It is) not modesty, nor decorum, nor honesty, nor timidity;—truly, the lack of a suitor, this (is) the cause of a woman's chastity.

Besides:—
127. A woman (is) like a jar of butter, a man (is) like glowing charcoal; therefore the wise should not place both butter and fire in one place.

Again:—
128. The father preserves in girlhood, the husband preserves in youth, and children (preserve) in the aged condition: a woman is not fit (for) liberty.

129. With mother, sister, or daughter, one should not be sitting sequestered; powerful (is) the aggregate of the senses, it draws even the wise (into danger).

Once, this Wanton, seated at her ease on a couch variegated with strings of jewels, (in) familiar intercourse with the merchant's son, the husband approached unperceived; seeing him (she) hastily arose, caught (him) by the hair, (and) ardently hugging, kissed (him); and hereupon the gallant got up (and) escaped. It is said:—

130. Whatever science Uśanas* knows, and whatever (science) Vrihaspati† knows; all that, even by nature, is firmly implanted in the understanding of women.

Seeing that embracing, a procuress, passing near, thought: Without cause she is embracing him. Afterwards, discovering the gallant (to be) the cause, Wanton was fined secretly by that procuress. Hence I say, "Suddenly a young wife," &c. Here there must be some cause sustaining the strength of the mouse. Having considered a moment, the mendicant said: And the reason here appears to be really the abundance of wealth. For:—

131. Every wealthy person in the world is everywhere always strong; even the power of kings arises, founded on wealth.

Then taking a pick-axe, (and) digging up the burrow, my long-hoarded wealth was seized by that mendicant. Then daily deprived of my strength, bereft of courage and energy, unable to obtain proper food, timidly and softly creeping about, I was seen by Tufted-ear. Then he said:

132. By wealth everyone (is) strong; from wealth one becomes wise; behold, this wicked mouse has attained the level of his species.

Again:—
133. All the acts of a man of little understanding, deprived (of) wealth, are destroyed, like rivulets in the hot season.

Moreover:—
134. Of whom (there are) riches, of him (there are) friends; of whom (there are) riches, of him (there are) relations; of whom (there are) riches, he (is) a man in the world; of whom (there are) riches, he (is) wise.

---

* The learned regent of the planet Venus; also, the author of a law-book, still extant.
† The preceptor of the gods, the ruler of speech and understanding.

Again:—

135. The house of the childless (is) empty, (so is the house) of one destitute of a true friend; for a fool the regions of space (are) empty; totally blank (is) poverty.

Verily:—

136. Between poverty and death, poverty is acknowledged the worse; death (is attended) with (but) little affliction; poverty (is) exceedingly hard to bear.

Besides:—

137. Those senses (are) unimpaired; so also (is) the name; this understanding (is) uninjured; so also (is) the voice:—deserted by the warmth of wealth, the man, of a truth, instantly becomes a different person.—Strange this.

Having heard all this I reflected: My remaining here (is) now improper; and as regards relating this incident to another, that also (is) improper.

For:—

138. A wise person should not divulge the loss of wealth, distress of mind, malpractices at home, the being cheated, and disgrace.

Also:—

139. Age, wealth, family dissension, private counsel, sexual intercourse, medicinal remedies, penance, almsgiving, and disgrace, (are) nine things to be carefully concealed.

And it is said:—

140. On fate (proving) exceedingly unpropitious, and on manliness being exerted in vain, whence, except from the forest,* (can there be) happiness for the sensible poor?

Again:—

141. A wise man dies pleasureably, but reaches not penury (pleasureably). Fire experiences even extinction, but approaches not coldness.

Moreover:—

142. As of a bunch of flowers, (there are) two states of a wise man; he should either remain on the head of all, or he should wither in the forest.

And as to living here by mendicancy, that (is) exceedingly despicable. For:—

143. Better the (funeral) fires were satisfied with the vital airs† by one deprived of wealth, (but) not the soliciting a churlish sordid person.

Besides:—

144. From poverty one reaches shame, overcome with shame he is deprived of spirit, (being) spirit-less he is despised, from contempt he approaches despondency, (being) despondent he goes on to misery, afflicted by misery he is deserted by intelligence, (being) sense-less he goes to destruction: alas! poverty (is) the seat of every calamity.

Moreover:—

145. Better (for) silence to be kept, but not a word uttered which (is) untrue; better impotency for me, but not intercourse with the wife of another; better the abandonment of life, but not delight in the words of a slanderer; better a subsistence on alms, but not the pleasure of feasting on another's wealth.

---

* *i.e.* voluntary banishment. † *i.e.* one were better dead.

146. Better an empty hall, but a wicked leader (is) certainly not good; better a harlot (for) wife, but not a re-married woman of (even) good family; better residence in the forest rather than in the city of a stupid king; better the abandonment of life rather than consorting among the vile.

Also :—

147. As service (takes away) all respect; as moonlight (removes) darkness; as old age, beauty; as tales of Vishṇu and S'iva, sin; so also beggary takes away a hundred (good) qualities.

Having reflected thus, how, afterwards, (shall) I feast myself with the food of another? O the wretchedness! that surely (were) a second Death's door!

For :—

148. Superficial learning, sexual intercourse purchased with a price, and subsisting subject to another, (are) three miseries of men.

Besides :—

149. The sick, the long exiled, the eater of another's food, the sleeper in another's house, what (part of life) he lives, that (is) death; what (is) death, that (is) his repose.

Though I reflected thus, still, from cupidity, again I made effort to take his food. Thus it is said :—

150. Through covetousness the intelligence wavers; covetousness begets insatiability; tormented with insatiability a man experiences misery here and in the other world.

Afterwards, struck by Lute-eared with that piece of split-cane, I reflected :—

151. One greedy of wealth, of unrestrained spirit, of unsubdued senses, (is) indeed discontented; truly every misfortune (is) his, of whom the mind (is) not contented.

In like manner :—

152. Every success (is) his, of whom the mind (is) contented; for one whose feet are covered with shoes (is) not the earth covered with leather?

Besides :—

153. What happiness (there is) for the tranquil-minded, satisfied with the nectar of content, whence (comes) such for those running hither and thither greedy of wealth?

Moreover :—

154. By him (everything) has been duly read, by him heard, (and) by him practised, who, having placed expectation behind his back, has relied upon non-expectancy.

And also :—

155. Happy (is) the life of anyone not spent at the door of the great, which has not experienced the pain of separation, (and) which has not uttered an unavailing word.

For :—

156. A hundred leagues (is) not far for one being borne along by desire; for the contented there is no regard for even the wealth held in the hand.

Therefore here the adoption of acts suitable to (one's) condition (is) best.

And it is said:

157. What (is) religion? Kindness to creatures. What (is) happiness? The healthiness of a living being in this world. What (is) kindness? Good nature. What (is) wisdom? Discrimination.

In like manner:—

158. Discrimination (is) indeed wisdom when a calamitous circumstance has occurred: for those incapable of exercising discrimination there are calamities step by step.

For instance:—

159. (A man) should abandon one (person) for the sake of a family; for the sake of a village he should abandon the family; the village (he should give up) for the sake of the country; for the sake of (his) soul he should abandon the earth.

Moreover:—

160. Either water without effort, or delicate fare followed by danger,—having well reflected (on this alternative) I perceive (that) that (is) happiness where (there is) repose.

Having reflected thus I am come to (this) deserted wood. For:—

161. Better a forest haunted by tigers and elephants, trees for shelter, ripe fruits and water for food, grass for a bed, bark for clothing; (but) not deprived of wealth, living amidst relations.

Afterwards, through the uprising of my good fortune, I have been favoured by this friend with a succession of favours; and now, by a continuation of good fortune, your Honour's protection, a very heaven, has been obtained by me. For:—

162. Of the poison-tree of the world (there are) indeed two sweet fruits,—the relish of the nectar of poetry, (and) association with good people.

Moreover:—

163. Society, the worship of Vishṇu, (and) immersion in the water of the Ganges, one should esteem three essential essences in (this) purely insipid world.

Torpid said:—

164. Riches (are) like the dust of the feet. Youth (is) like the rush of a mountain torrent. Manhood (is) fickle (and) unsteady as a drop of water. Life (is) like foam. He who with unwavering mind does not perform the duties (which are) the key of the gate of heaven, struck with remorse (and) bent down with decay, he is consumed by the fire of grief.

An excessive accumulation was made by you; that (was) your fault. Listen:—

165. The very abandonment of accumulated riches (is) really (their) preservation; as a pipe (is) of the waters stored in a tank.

Besides:—

166. The wealth which the miser buried deep down in the earth, that constructed before-hand a path to reach a mansion below.

For:—

167. He who, obstructing his own happiness seeks the accumulation of wealth, like the bearer of another's goods, he is a vessel of misery.

Thus it is said:—

168. If (we are) rich with the wealth deprived of liberality and enjoyment; then

we (are) rich with the wealth buried in the caves of the earth.

169. (He) of whom the days pass without giving (or) enjoying, he though puffing like a blacksmith's bellows, does not live.

170. What (profits one) with wealth who neither gives nor enjoys? and what, with strength, who does not repel enemies? and what, with learning, who does not practise religion? what, with a soul, who has not conquered his senses?

Moreover :—

171. Through non-enjoyment (there is) common property in wealth, of a miser with others. "This (was) his," such connection (with it), on (its) loss, is attained with misery.*

Also :—

172. Neither to God, nor to a Bráhman, nor to relations, nor to himself, does the wealth of a miser go. By fire, thieves, (or) the king (it is consumed).

Moreover :—

173. Distribution, enjoyment, (and) loss, are the three courses of wealth; the third course is his who neither gives, nor enjoys.

And it has been said :—

174. Liberality with kindly speech, knowledge without pride, bravery followed by compassion, and wealth accompanied by its abandonment;—these four excellencies (are) hard to be found.

And it is said :—

175. Accumulation should always be made, excessive accumulation should not be made; behold, that jackal of acquisitive disposition was killed by a bow.

Well-to-do said: How (was) that? Torpid relates (as follows): There was a hunter named Terrible, resident in the village of Prosperity; and he once (being) desirous of meat, taking (his) bow, went into the Vindhya-forest. There a deer was killed by him. Having taken the deer, while going along he saw a pink-eyed boar of an awful form. Then having placed the deer on the earth, the boar was hit by him with a very sharp arrow; also, by the boar approaching, making a roar dreadful as the clouds at the dissolution of the universe, the hunter was struck in the groin, whereby he fell on the earth, like a tree cut down. For :—

176. Water, fire, poison, a weapon, hunger, sickness, a fall from a precipice;—having met some cause or other, a corporeal being is deserted by the vital airs.

Now by the trampling of both their feet, a serpent also was killed. Hereupon a jackal named Long-yell, wandering about in quest of food, saw these dead ones, the deer, hunter, serpent, and boar. Having perceived them he reflected: O the luck! a great feast is ready for me. For :—

177. Just as, for corporeal beings, unthought-of troubles are coming, so also (come) pleasures. I think fortune is here predominant.

Be it so (or not), with the flesh of these, three months will pass pleasurably for me.

---

* Wealth unenjoyed is as much the property of a stranger as it is of the owner; on its being lost, the connection of ownership is attended with a pain (which, of course, the stranger never experiences).

178. The man goes to one month; two months, the deer and the boar; the serpent goes for one day; to-day is to be eaten the string of the bow.

Therefore, in the first cravings of hunger I (will) eat this unsavoury sinewy thong attached to the notch of the bow. Having said this, he did so. On that sinewy thong being severed, by the bow quickly springing up, Long-yell was pierced in the heart, (and) immediately attained the five-fold state.* Hence I say, "Accumulation is always to be made," &c.

So also :—

179. What he gives (and) what he enjoys, that truly (is) the wealth of the wealthy; others sport with the wife and with the riches of the deceased.

180. What thou givest to excellent persons, and what thou eatest day by day, that (is) thy wealth, I think;—(what) thou art keeping (is) the hoard of someone else.

Let that pass now; what (advantage will arise) with extended description? For :—

181. Philosophic-minded men desire not the unattainable, they are not inclined to bemoan the lost, they are not perplexed even in calamities.

Therefore, friend, thou shouldst be ever energetic. For :—

182. Even after studying the scriptures they are fools, but he who (is) practical, he (is) the wise man. A well-devised medicine does not effectuate the health of those in pain, with the name merely.

Besides :—

183. For one afraid of exertion, a precept of wisdom effectuates not even the smallest advantage. For a blind person, what object in this world does a lamp make clear, although standing on the palm of (his) hand?

Therefore here, O friend! under existing circumstances tranquillity should be maintained.

184. One should attend to pleasure (which) has come, also trouble (which) has happened: troubles and pleasures revolve like a wheel.

Moreover :—

185. All riches unresistingly approach the energetic man; as frogs, the pool, (and) as fish, the full lake.

Also :—

186. Prosperity voluntarily goes, for an abiding place, (to) one endowed with resolution, unprocrastinating, conversant with right principles of action, unaddicted to vices, valorous, grateful, and firm in friendship.

And especially :—

187. Even without riches the firm (man) reaches a position of much honour and elevation; a mean (person), though endowed with riches, attains the status of contempt. Can a dog, although wearing a golden collar, acquire the naturally lofty dignity inherent in a lion, having for object the acquisition of a multitude of (good) qualities?

Moreover :—

188. "(I am) wealthy," (this is) thy pride. What? (thy) wealth being gone art

---

* *i.e.*, was resolved into the five elements, earth, air, fire, water, and ether; that is to say, he died.

thou approaching despondency? The falls and risings of men (are) like a hand-tossed ball.

Besides:—

189. The shadow of a cloud, the friendship of the base, new corn, women, youthful pleasures, and riches, (are) to be enjoyed for a certain time (only).

Moreover:—

190. One should not strive excessively for a subsistence,—that, verily, has been provided by the Creator;—as soon as a living being has dropped from the womb, both teats of the mother stream.

Listen, O friend!

191. He by whom swans were made white, and parrots were made green, and by whom peacocks were diversified (in colour), he will provide thy subsistence.

And hear another secret of the good, O friend!

192. They engender trouble in (their) acquisition, they inflict pain in disasters, and they perplex in prosperity;—how (then, are) riches vehicles of happiness?

Besides:—

193. The absence of desire (is) better for anyone that the desire of wealth for (even) religious purposes. The non-contact of mud, (by keeping) aloof, (is) better than washing (it) off.

For:—

194. As flesh is devoured by birds in the sky, by beasts on the earth, by fishes in the water; in a similar manner, a rich man (is devoured) everywhere.

Moreover:—

195. From the king, from flood, from fire, from robbery, from even their own folk, there is continual fear for the wealthy; as (there is fear) of death for living creatures.

In like manner:—

196. In a life abounding with troubles, what greater than (this) misery (can there be)?—from which, the accomplishment of the wish is not, (and still) where the wish ceases not.

Again, O brother! hear:—

197. Wealth at first (is) not easily acquired; (when) acquired it is preserved with difficulty; the loss of what has been acquired (is) like death; therefore one should not be anxious about it.

198. If this thirst were renounced who (would be) poor? who rich? If its course is allowed, slavery is placed on the head.

Moreover:—

199. Whatsoever has been desired, from that (fresh) desire proceeds; that object is really obtained wealth from which desire ceases.

What (advantage will accrue) with much (argumentation)? With affectionate conversation, let the time be passed here with me. For:—

200. The friendships of the magnanimous last till death, (their) resentments (are) vanishing momentarily; and (their) liberality (is) without self-interest.

Having heard this Gently-alighting says: Happy art thou, O Torpid! thou art ever to be resorted to (for protection). For:—

201. The good truly (are) always able to bear the misfortunes of the good; of a truth, elephants (are) the burden-bearers of elephants sunk in the mire.

And also:—
202. One appreciative of virtue delights in a virtuous person; for one viciously disposed (there is) no satisfaction in a virtuous person. A bee goes from the wood (to) the lotus; but not so a frog, although a co-habitant.

Again:—
203. He (is) the one to be praised on the earth, among human beings he (is) the best,—a real man,—he (is) fortunate,—whose suppliants or refugees are not departing disappointed in hopes (and) face-averted.

Then, in this manner, they, feeding and rambling at their own pleasure, lived at ease contented. Now once (upon a time) a deer named Dapple-body startled by somebody came there (and) joined (them). Then, supposing (that) the cause of the alarm was coming after, Torpid entered the water, and the mouse went (to his) burrow, the crow flying up perched on the top of a tree. Then Gently-alighting, after looking a great distance, discovered no cause of fear whatever. Having come back, again all met together (and) sat down. Torpid said: Friend deer! prosperity to thee! according to thy desire let provender of water, &c., be enjoyed! by residing here let this wood be made to own a master! Says Dapple-body: Alarmed by a hunter I am come (to) the protection of your honours. For:—

204. Should one abandon, either from avarice or from fear, one come for protection, the wise have declared his sin (to be) equal to killing a Brâhman.

And therefore I desire friendship with your honours. Well-to-do said: As to that, the friendship of your honour with us (is) accomplished without effort. For:—

205. A friend (is) to be regarded (as of) four kind,—one's own offspring, also one formed by connection, one come in the line of the family, one rescued from misfortunes.

Here, then, stay, without difference from your own home. Having heard this, the deer delighted fed at his pleasure, drank the water, (and) sat in the shade of a tree near the lake. For:—

206. Well-water, the shade of the fig-tree, a dark woman, (and) a brick house, in cold weather should be warm, and in warm weather cold.

Now Torpid says: Friend deer! by whom wast thou alarmed? In this deserted wood what hunters ever are roaming? The deer replied: There is, in the country of Kalinga, a king named Gold-armlet; and he, having arrived, in the course of (his) occupation of subjugating districts, is encamped on the banks of the river Moon's-portion; but early (to-morrow), advancing here, he (is) to be in the vicinity of lake Camphor,—thus, from the mouth of hunters, the rumour is heard. Therefore, considering the abiding hereabout (till) the morning a cause of alarm, let what should be done be commenced. Hearing that, the tortoise timidly said: Friend! I am going (to) another water-tank. The crow and deer also both said: Friend, let it be so.

Well-to-do, having reflected, said: On again having attained a water-tank (there is) safety for Torpid; what kind (of safety is there) for his going on land? For :—

207. The chief strength of aquatic animals (is) the waters; of residents in strongholds, a fortress; of beasts of prey, their own ground; of kings, an army.

Friend Gently-alighting! by this counsel it will be thus—

208. As the merchant's son, having himself seen (his) wife's budding bosom pressed, became pained, just so thou wilt be.

They said: How (was) that? Well-to-do relates (as follows): There is in the country of Hump-backed-girls, a king named Heroic-host. By him, in a town named Hero-city, the prince called Exalted-might was made viceroy. And he (was) very rich (and) handsome. Once (while) perambulating his city he perceived the wife of a merchant's son named Loveliness, (in) the full flower of youth. Then, having gone home, (his) mind distressed by passion, he sent a female messenger for her.

For :—
209. So long he continues in a good course, just so long a man has the mastery of the passions, so long he shows modesty, just so long even he maintains decorum,—as long as these arrows of the eyes of wanton women, drawn and shot from the bow of the eye-brow, reaching the ear, feathered with black, stealing the steadfastness, fall not upon the heart.

Loveliness also, from the moment of seeing him, with heart split by the blow of love's arrow, became fixed in thought upon him. And thus it is said :—

210. Untruthfulness, precipitancy, delusion, envy, and excessive avarice, want of principle, (and) impurity, (are) the innate faults of women.

Now, having heard the messenger's discourse, Loveliness said: How (can) I engage in this wickedness, transgressing (against my) husband? I, faithful to (my) lord, do not so much as touch another man. For :—

211. She (is) a wife who (is) clever in the house; she (is) a wife who (is) prolific; she (is) a wife who (is her) husband's life; she (is) a wife who (is) faithful.

212. Of cuckoos the voice (is) the beauty; woman's beauty (is) faithfulness; knowledge (is) the beauty of the ugly; patience (is) the beauty of ascetics.

Again :—
213. She (is) not to be styled a wife in whom the husband delights not; when the husband of women is pleased, all the deities should be satisfied.

Therefore whatever my life's lord points out, even that I unhesitatingly do. The messenger said: (Is) that true? Loveliness replied: Indeed that (is) certainly true.

Then all that had been said by Loveliness, the messenger departing related before Exalted-might. Hearing that, Exalted-might said: Heart-stricken by Vishameshu,* without her how shall I live? The procuress said: Brought by (her) husband, (she) should be surrendered (to you). He exclaimed: How (is) that possible? The procuress replied: Let stratagem be employed. For:—

214. Truly that (is) possible by stratagem which (is) not possible by prowess; by a jackal going along a miry road, an elephant was killed.

The prince asks: How (was) that? She relates (as follows):—There is in the forest of Brahma an elephant named Camphor-marked; having seen him all the jackals reflected (thus): If he by any means were to die, then with his body there would be four months' desirable provision for us. Thereupon, from among them, an old jackal made (this) promise: His death is to be accomplished by me through the energy of (my) intelligence. Accordingly the deceiver, going near to Camphor-marked, fell prostrate (and) reverentially said: Sire! grant the favour of a look. Says the elephant: Who (art) thou? whence (art thou) come? He replied: I (am) a jackal, by all the assembled beasts, dwellers in the forest, despatched to your honour. Since to remain without a king (is) not proper, therefore your honour, endowed with every princely virtue, has been selected to be here inaugurated in the sovereignty of the forest. For:—

215. (He who is) immaculate by (reason of) family duties and social duties, majestic, just, (and) skilful in polity, he is fit (to be) a ruler in the earth.

Observe further:—

216. First one should find a king, then a wife, then wealth; on the non-existence of a king in this world, whence a wife? whence wealth?

Besides:—

217. Like a cloud, a king (is) the sustainer of creatures; even on the failing of a cloud one may live, but not on a king (failing).

Moreover:—

218. In this (one-to-)another-subject† world, for the most part one abides in his proper sphere through the application of punishment; (for) a virtuous person (is) hard to be found. Through fear of punishment a virtuous woman obeys (her) husband, although (he be) weak or failing, or sick or poor.

Therefore having so acted that the auspicious time does not pass away, let your Majesty come quickly. Having said this (he) arose (and) departed. Then this Camphor-marked, drawn by the lust of sovereignty, running along the road indicated by the jackal, sank into a great bog. The elephant called out: Friend jackal! what (is) now to be done? I, fallen in a great bog, am dying. Turn back (and) see. The jackal laughingly said: Sire! apply (your) trunk on the tip of my tail (and) get up. This (is) the recompense of him on whose word confidence was placed by thee. And thus it is said:—

219. As often as thou shalt be deprived of the society of the good, so often wilt thou fall among companies of the wicked.

---

* The god with odd arrows, the Indian Cupid being supposed to be armed with five arrows.
† In which one person is subject to another person throughout all stages of society.

Then the elephant sunk in a great bog was devoured by the jackals. Hence I say: "What is possible by merely a stratagem," &c. Then by the advice of the procuress, the prince made that merchant's son named Pretty-gift (his) servant. Then this (servant) was employed by him in all confidential matters. Once, by advice of the procuress, the prince, anointed after bathing (and) wearing golden ornaments, said: O Pretty-gift, by me, during one month, a vow to Gaurî should be performed; therefore, beginning to-day, bring (and) consign (to me) every night a young woman of (good) family; and she shall be honoured by me with due ceremony. Accordingly Pretty-gift, bringing a young woman of that description, presents (her); afterwards, being secreted, he watches to see what he would do.* But Exalted-might, without even touching the young woman, having done homage at a distance, with clothes, ornaments, perfumes, and sandal, (and) having provided a guard, dismissed (her) immediately. Now that having been seen by the merchant's son, with the confidence engendered (and) with mind attracted by avarice, his own wife was brought (and) presented. But Exalted-might, having recognised Loveliness, the delight of his heart, hastily having arisen, ardently embraced (her, his) eyes expanded with joy, (his) heart delighted, indulging in many kinds of amorous dalliance, he sported with her on the couch. Having seen this, the merchant's son, (motionless) as a picture, bewildered as to what was to be done, experienced excessive dejection. So also, will it be with thee. However, disregarding that speech, with great trepidation Torpid, quitting (his) watery asylum, started off. Well-to-do and the others, from friendship apprehensive of (something) disagreeable, followed him. Presently, whilst going on dry land, Torpid was caught by a certain hunter scouring the wood. And he having captured him, picked (him) up, fastened (him) on (his) bow, (and) saying "I am lucky," started towards his own house. Now the deer, crow, and mouse, experiencing extreme dejection, followed after him. Then Well-to-do mourned:—

220. Ere I reach the end of one trouble like the further shore of the ocean, lo, a second (trouble) is ready. For my faults, troubles are multiplied.

221. He who (is) a natural-born friend is truly produced by good fortune; his inartificial friendship, even among misfortunes, he renounces not. For:—

222. Not in a mother, nor in a wife, nor in a full brother, nor in a son, (is there) such confidence for a man, as (there is) in a natural-born friend.

Having reflected thus repeatedly, (he exclaimed), Alas, my ill-luck! For:—

223. The effects of the offspring of my own acts, both good and bad, occurring after intervals of time,—even in this world, these different conditions have been experienced by me, like different births.

But even so it (is) :—
224. The body (is) near its dissolution; successes (are) the seat of misfortunes; meetings have (their) departures; all that springs up (is) evanescent.

---

* *Lit.* "What is he doing?" thus he watches.

Again having reflected, he said :—

225. By whom was created this two-syllable jewel "Mitram,"* the preserver from sorrows, enemies, and fears, the depository of affection and confidence ?

Moreover :—

226. The friend who may be the elixir-like delight of the eyes, the joy of the heart, the participator of pleasure and pain with a friend, he (is) hard to be acquired; but others, friends in the time of prosperity, filled with the greed of pelf, they are everywhere to be found :—but their touchstone (is) affliction.

Thus having deeply lamented Well-to-do said to Dapple-body and Gently-alighting : Ere this hunter passes out from the wood, let an effort be made to release Torpid. They replied : Quickly point out what is to be done. Well-to-do says : Let Dapple-body, having gone near the water, make himself appear motionless, as if dead ; and let the crow, placing (himself) above him, scratch somewhat with (his) beak. Assuredly, the hunter, desirous of venison, having left the tortoise there, will hastily approach ; then I will sever the bond of Torpid. Thereupon Dapple-body and Gently-alighting having hastily gone, upon its being done as agreed the weary hunter, having drunk water (and) being seated under a tree, in the manner indicated having perceived the deer, placing the tortoise near the water (and) taking a hunting-knife, with a joyful heart went towards the deer. In the interim the tortoise (whose) bond had been severed by Well-to-do, (who) had approached (him), hastily entered the water; and the deer, seeing the hunter close by, sprang up (and) quickly fled away. When the hunter, turning back, approaches the foot of the tree, then not seeing the tortoise he reflected (thus) : This is just the fitting (recompense) for my incircumspect acting. For :—

227. Whoever, quitting certainties, pursues uncertainties, his certainties are being lost, (and) the uncertainties are actually lost.

He then, through his own act, entered the village disconsolate ; and Torpid and the rest, all free from danger, went to their own place, and remained with corresponding happiness. Now the Princes joyfully said : We have heard all, we (are) delighted ; our desire has been accomplished. Vishṇuśarman replied : With this much the wish of your Honours has been realized ; and may this other also:—

228. May you, the good, acquire a friend ! May prosperity be obtained by populous communities ! May kings continually firm in their duty, nourish the earth ! May your Policy endure for the gratification of the mind of the virtuous, like a newly-wed wife ! May the revered Half-moon-Crested one† effect the prosperity of the people !

Here ends the first chapter, called " the Acquisition of Friends," in the "Friendly Advice " collected by Vishṇuśarman.

---

* " A friend." † The God S'iva.

SEPARATION OF FRIENDS.

Afterwards the Princes said: Sir, the "Acquisition of Friends" has been heard thus far by us, now we are desirous to hear the "Separation of Friends." Vishṇuśarman replied: Let the "Separation of Friends" be heard, of which this (is) the first verse:—

1. The great and increasing friendship of a lion and a bull, in a wood, was destroyed by an envious and very greedy jackal.

The Princes said: How (was) that? Vishṇuśarman relates (as follows): On the southern road* there is a city named Golden; (and) there a very wealthy merchant, named Prospering, dwells. Although his wealth was ample, (yet) seeing others (his) relatives extremely opulent, (his) opinion was that a further increase of wealth should be effected. For:—

2. Whose greatness is not enhanced (by) looking lower and lower? Of a truth all are becoming poor (by) looking higher and higher.

Moreover:—
3. A man of whom there is abundant wealth is honoured, even the murderer of a Brahman; although equal in race to the Moon, (if) penniless he is despised.

Again:—
4. The non-persevering, the lazy, the fatalist, and one destitute of courage, Prosperity does not desire to embrace; just, indeed, as a young woman (does not desire to embrace) an old husband.

Moreover:—
5. Laziness, uxuriousness, sickness, tenderness for one's native place, contentment, (and) timidity, (are) the six obstacles to greatness.

For:—
6. He who is content with even very little wealth,—Providence, I think, having done what was to have been done,† does not increase that (wealth) for him.

Moreover:—
7. May no woman whatever give birth to such a son as this—unenergetic, cheerless, non-courageous, the delight of his enemies.

Thus truly has it been said:—
8. One should desire to gain (what is yet) unobtained; one should preserve with care (what) has been obtained; one should increase properly (what) has been preserved; one should spend upon places of pilgrimage (what) has been increased.

And unincreasing wealth, in time, with even very little expenditure, like collyrium, goes to waste; and (the wealth) not being enjoyed (is) wholly useless.

---

* *i.e.* the Dakkhan.   † *i.e.* having made him contented.

Thus, indeed, has been said:—

9. Having observed the wasting of collyrium, and the increasing of an ant-hill, one should make time fruitful, with alms-giving, study, and (virtuous) acts.

For:—

10. A pitcher is filled gradually by falling drops of water: this (is) the cause of all sciences, of religion, and of wealth.

Having thus reflected, Prospering, having attached two bulls, named Lively and Gladdening, to the pole, (and) having laden (his) cart with various kinds of goods, started towards Kashmîr for traffic. For:—

11. What (is) an excessive burden for the powerful? what (is) distant for the enterprizing? what (is) foreign for the educated? who (is) a stranger for those who speak kindly?

Now going along, in the great forest called Hard-to-pass, Lively fell down (and) broke his knees; seeing that, Prospering (then) reflected:

12. Truly, let the prudent man act energetically hither and thither; still the result will be just that which rested in the mind of the Creator.

Moreover:—

13. Dismay, the obstacle to all enterprizes, (is) by all means to be eschewed; therefore, having discarded dismay, success in what is to be accomplished is attained.

Having thus reflected, leaving Lively there, Prospering went on. Lively, also, somehow or other resting (his) weight on three hoofs, remained there in the forest. For:—

14. The (allotted) age preserves the vital members of one plunged in the abyss of the ocean, of one fallen from a mountain, (and) of one bitten by even a venomous snake.

Moreover:—

15. Though pierced by a hundred arrows at the wrong time an animal dies not; touched by only the point of a blade of grass, at the appointed time, he lives not.

16. An unguarded object remains (safe, if) protected by destiny; stricken by destiny it perishes (though) well guarded. One lives, though abandoned in a wood without a protector; one lives not in a house, though precaution be taken.

Afterwards, as the days were passing, Lively, by the obtention of food, &c., such as he desired, roaming the woods frisky and fat bellowed lustily. In that wood, a lion named Tawny remained enjoying the pleasure of sovereignty acquired by his own arm. As it is said:—

17. No inauguration, nor consecration, is performed by beasts for the lion: lordship over brutes (is) the natural right of him who has acquired the sovereignty by prowess.

He [the lion] once, distressed by thirst, went to the banks of the Jumna to drink water; and there, the bellowing of Lively, hitherto unexperienced by the lion, was heard by him, like the roar of thunder-clouds at the dissolution of the universe. Hearing that, without drinking the water, alarmedly retreating, (and) returning to his own place, reflecting on what it could be, (he) remained silent; and in this condition he was seen by two jackals, named Karaṭaka and Damanaka, the sons of his minister. Seeing him in that plight, Damanaka said to Karaṭaka: "Friend Karaṭaka, how (is it) that this (our) master, being desirous of water, withdraws stealthily without drinking the water?" Karaṭaka says: "Friend Damanaka, with my concurrence service is not performed for him; therefore what (advantage will result) by investigating his actions? for great trouble is endured by us two through being neglected by this king.

18. Behold what is done by servants seeking wealth by service,—whatever personal independence (they possess), even that is lost by the blockheads.

Moreover:—
19. They who (are) the dependants of another suffer cold, wind, heat, and fatigue; even with a fraction of it a wise man doing penance, might be blest.

Again:—
20. As much as independence (extends) so far is birth profitable; (if) those who are (in) subjection to others live, who (are) dead?

Moreover:—
21. "Come, go, fall, stand up, speak, keep silence,"—in this way the wealthy sport with the needy, held in the grasp of expectancy.

Moreover:—
22. Idiots adorning themselves carefully make themselves subservient to others, for the acquisition of pelf; just (as is done) by harlots.

Again:—
23. Servants esteem highly even the look of (their) master,—which (being) by its very nature fickle, falls also upon the impure.

And especially:—
24. He stoops for the sake of rising; for the sake of living he resigns (his) breath; he becomes miserable for the sake of pleasure. Who (is) a greater fool than a servant?

Moreover:—
25. From silence (he is esteemed) a fool; (if) eloquent, (he is) crazy or a chatterbox; by patience (he is thought) timid; if he cannot bear (patiently, he is) for the most part not well-bred; he remains at (your) side, (then he is) certainly impudent (and) from (keeping) distant, (he is) irresolute;—the most embarrassing duty of a servant is unattainable even for Yogins."[*]

Damanaka said: "Friend, such things are by no means to be done even mentally.

26. How, forsooth, are not those great lords to be diligently served, who, in a very short (time), when satisfied, satisfy the wishes of the heart?

Moreover:—
27. Whence (can come) the exalted honours of the chaurí,[†] the upraised white umbrella, the horse, the elephant, and the carriage,— for those destitute of employ?"

---

[*] Saints who have acquired supernatural power.   [†] Part of the insignia of royalty.

Says Karaṭaka: "Still what (have we to do) with this (which is) not our affair? Interference in affairs with which one has no concern must be avoided by all means. For:—

28. The man who desires to interfere in affairs which do not concern him, lies struck down on the earth, like the monkey who pulled out the wedge."

Damanaka asked: "How (was) that?" Karaṭaka relates (as follows): There was in the country of Magadha, on land in the vicinity of the forest of Virtue, a pleasure-house begun to be built by a man of the writer-caste, named Auspiciously-given. There, between the two parts, split up a little way, of a wooden post (that was) being cut up by a saw, a wedge had been inserted by the carpenter. There (also) a large herd of monkeys inhabiting the wood came for pastime. One monkey among them, as though sent by the wand of Fate, grasping that wedge with both hands sat down; then his testicles hanging down entered between the two pieces of wood. Hereupon, with his natural restlessness, with a great effort he pulled the wedge; and, upon the wedge being drawn out, both testicles being crushed by the two pieces of wood, he perished. Hence I say: "Interference in affairs which do not concern one," &c. Damanaka said: "Nevertheless, an investigation into the actions of a master should surely be made by a servant." Karaṭaka replied: "He who is engaged in general superintendence (is) prime-minister; let him do it; for interference in the department of others should not be attempted by a subordinate. Behold:—

29. He who should interfere in the department of another, through desire to benefit (his) master, he rues it; like the donkey beaten through braying."

Damanaka asked: "How (was) that?" Karaṭaka related (as follows):—There is, in Benares, a washerman named Camphor-cloth; and he once, having sported for a long time with his very young wife, slept soundly. Hereupon a certain thief entered his house to steal the goods. In his court-yard a donkey was standing tied up, and a dog was sitting. Perceiving that thief, the donkey said (to) the dog: "This (is) your affair; then how (is it) thou art not awakening the master by making a loud noise?" Says the dog: "It behoves thee not to trouble about this business; thou knowest how I protect this (fellow's) house, hence he, for a long time free from care, does not know my value, so that now (he is) remiss even in giving my food; without the appearance of (some) d nger, masters become inattentive (to) their dependants." Says the ass: "Listen, blockhead—

30. What servant (and) what friend (is) he who makes demands in the time for action?"

The dog rejoins:—

"What master (is) he who, in the time for work, should not maintain servants?

Moreover:—

31. In the maintenance of attendants, in the service of a master, in the practice of virtue, and in the begetting of a son, there are no proxies."

Then the ass angrily said: "Ah! most wicked (art) thou who art neglecting (thy) master's affairs. Well, I must so act that the master (will) awake. For :—

32. One should serve the sun with the back; fire, with the belly; a master, with all the soul; (and) the next world, with sincerity."

Having said this, he brayed excessively. Then the washerman, aroused by that noise, getting up enraged at the disturbance of (his) slumbers, beat the ass with a stick. Through that beating the ass perished. Hence I say, "Interference in the department of another," &c. See, the searching after beasts (is) our affair; therefore, let (us) be busy about our own employment. Having reflected (he continued)—But to-day no advantage (can arise) by even thy solicitude (on this account); since abundant leavings of food remain for us two." Damanaka angrily said : "How, art thou serving the king merely for the sake of food? That was unbecomingly uttered by a servant. For :—

33. For the sake of the assisting of friends, also for the sake of the injuring of enemies, the favour of a monarch is desired by the wise. Who does not merely nourish the belly?

34. In the life of whom, Brâhmans, friends, and relations live, his life (is) profitable. Who does not live for himself?

Besides :—

35. But let him live, in whom, living, many live. Does not even the crow fill his own belly with (his) beak?

Behold :—

36. One man goes (to) servitude for five purânas*; another, clever one, for hundreds of thousands; another is not obtained for even hundreds of thousands.

For :—

37. In the equal human race service is exceedingly degrading. Who (is) not the first there, even he is reckoned among the (merely) living.

Thus it is said :—

38. Between a horse, an elephant, and iron; between wood, stone, and clothes; between women, men, and water ;—the difference (is) a great difference.

For instance :—

39. A dog having obtained even a fleshless bone, smeared with fat, with a few sinews, attains delight, but it (may) not (suffice) to the satisfaction of his hunger ;—the lion, quitting the jackal already (in his) grasp, slays the elephant. Every person, though reduced to difficulties, desires again according to his nature.

Further, behold the difference between the server and the served—

40. A dog wags his tail, crouches down at the feet, and falling on the ground shows his face and belly, for the giver of a mouthful; but the noble elephant looks gravely, and (only) with a hundred coaxings, eats.

---

* Small coins.

Moreover:—

41. Even an instant lived here, renowned by men, (as) being associated with learning, valour, and fame, *that* the knowing call truly living. Even a crow lives for a long time, and eats the offerings.*

Moreover:—

42. What (is) the difference between a brute and the beast of a man (whose) reason is devoid of the discrimination between evil and good, (who is) excluded by many (conversant) with sacred affairs, (and who is) desirous merely of filling his belly?

Says Karaṭaka: "Both of us, at least, (are) without authority; then what have we (to do) with this affair?" Damanaka replied: "In how little time may a minister attain supremacy or subordination! For:—

43. No one in this world becomes esteemed, (either) respected of any, or vile; in the world, his own actions lead a man (to) dignity or disgrace.

Moreover:—

44. As by a great effort a stone is raised on a hill, and is made to descend down instantaneously, so the soul in virtue and vice (ascends and descends).

Therefore, friend, dependent on self-effort (is) the soul of everyone.

45. A man by his own acts goes down and down, (or) moves upwards; just as the digger of a well, or the builder of a wall."

"Now," said Karaṭaka, "what is your Honour (about to) say?" Damanaka replied: "This master Tawny from fear from some quarter, without drinking the water, has timidly returned, and is seated (at home)."

Karaṭaka asked: "How art thou knowing that?"

Damanaka replied: "What is unknown to the wise? It is said:—

46. The uttered meaning is apprehended even by a brute; horses and elephants (when) bidden move forwards; a wise person guesses what is even not uttered. (Acute) intellects (are) successful in understanding the gestures of others.

Besides:—

47. By external appearances, by gestures, by the gait, by a movement, by a word, by a change of eye (or) mouth, the inward thought is indicated.

So here, on an occasion (arising from his) fear, I, by aid of my knowledge, will make him my own. For:—

48. He is wise who knows the speech suitable to the occasion, the affection appropriate to the good-nature (of the recipient), and resentment proportioned to his strength."

Karaṭaka (then) said: "Friend, thou art ignorant of service. Behold:—

49. He who should enter uncalled, (who) speaks much unasked, (and) thinks himself a favourite of the king,—he (is) dull-witted."

Damanaka asked: "Friend, how (am) I ignorant of service? Behold:—

50. Is there anything naturally beautiful or not beautiful? Whatever is pleasing to anyone, that (is) beautiful for him.

---

* Accounted a discreditable manner of subsistence.

Moreover :—

51. Whatever (be) the natural disposition of anyone, a wise man, having insinuated (himself) by that quickly leads that man (into) his own power.

Again :—

52. "Who (is) here?" (having heard this) "I," he should say, and "Command (me) wholly." To the utmost of his ability he should execute the exact command of the king.

Moreover :—

53. Desiring little, steadfast, wise, always following like a shadow, not hesitating (when) commanded,—he may dwell in the king's palace."

"Suppose," says Karaṭaka, "the master is displeased with thee for unseasonable intrusion?"

Damanaka replied: "Let it be so; still an attendant should certainly present (himself). For :—

54. Non-commencement from fear of (committing) a fault, (is) the mark of a coward. O brother, by whom is food renounced from fear of indigestion?

Behold :—

55. The king favours the man (who is) near (him, though) unlearned, of low family, or unpolished; for the most part, kings, women, and tendrils, entwine around him who remains at (their) side."

Karaṭaka asked: "Now having gone there, what (wilt) thou say?"

Damanaka said: "Listen; I will just ascertain (this : is) the master favourable or unfavourable (to) me?"

Karaṭaka asked: "What (is) the sign for ascertaining that?"

Damanaka replied: "Listen.

56. A look from a distance, an exceedingly courteous smile on inquiry, the praise of qualities even in (one's) absence, (and) remembrance among agreeable things.

57. Attachment to one not serving, liberality, increasing affection, the remembrance of virtues even on a fault (being committed), are the signs of an attached master.

58. Procrastinating, the raising hopes, the withholding rewards,—a wise man would recognize (as) the signs of a disaffected master.

Having ascertained that, I will speak so that he shall become subservient (to) me. Since :—

59. The wise are exhibiting,—as if bursting forth (as) the result of the precepts of polity,—disaster arising from the exhibition of helplessness, (and) success arising from the exhibition of contrivance.

Moreover :—

60. Qualities (are) of three kinds in (the estimation of) a master; faults (are) virtues, virtues (are) faults, faults (are) faults (and) virtues (are) virtues,—in (the opinion of) an attached, estranged, (and) impartial (master respectively)."

Says Karaṭaka: "Nevertheless, on an opportunity not occurring thou shouldst not speak. For :—

61. Even Vrihaspati* uttering an unseasonable speech would incur contempt (for his) understanding, and eternal disgrace."

---

* See p. 21.

Damanaka replied: "Friend, do not fear. I will not utter an unseasonable speech. For:—

62. In calamity, in straying from the road, and on the opportunities for action passing away, a servant desiring (his master's) good should speak, even unasked.

And if upon a proper opportunity counsel is not to be uttered by me, then, truly, my ministerial office (is) worthless. For:—

63. That quality by which one obtains a living, and by which one is praised by the good in the world, ought to be preserved and increased by its possessor.

Therefore, friend, permit (me to) go to Tawny."
Karaṭaka exclaimed: "May it be fortunate! May the result be as desired!

64. May (you) go for the acquisition of wealth, for prosperity, for conquest, for the destruction of the enemies faction, and for a (safe) return!"

Then Damanaka, as if amazed, went to Tawny. Now seen by the king even from afar, (and) allowed to enter, (the jackal) having reverentially saluted him, sat down.
The King said: "Thou art seen after a long (interval)."
Damanaka replied: "Although for the feet of your revered Highness there is no need whatever (of) me (your) servant, still, on a suitable occasion, a dependant should surely present (himself); (hence) I am come.

65. O king! the work of grandees is (done) by a straw, for the picking of the teeth or for the tickling of the ear; how (much more can be done) by a man possessed of body, speech, and hands.

Although a loss of intelligence in long-despised me is suspected by (my) master, still it (is) not the fact. For:—

66. A jewel dangles at the feet; glass is placed on the head. At the time of buying and selling, glass (is) glass, a gem (is) a gem. Again:—

67. Loss of intelligence is not to be apprehended (in) one of resolute habits, although ill-treated. A flame of fire though reversed never goes downwards.

Sire, by all means a master should be discriminative. For:—

68. When a king indiscriminately acts to all alike, then the efforts of those capable of exertion is prostrated. Moreover:—

69. Men (are) of three kinds, O king! superior, inferior, (and) middling; thus, therefore, he should employ them in three kinds of work. For:—

70. In (their) proper place, both servants and ornaments are becoming: a crest-jewel (is) not (worn) on the foot, nor an ankle-ring on the head. Besides:—

71. If a jewel worth placing in a golden ornament is set in lead, it neither tinkles

nor shines; (this) is the fault of the setter.

Again:—

72. (If) glass (be) mounted on a crown, and a jewel on a foot-ornament, it is not the fault of the jewel, but the gaffer's ignorance.

Observe:—

73. "This (is) an intelligent fellow; (that) a faithful one; here (is) one (possessed of) both qualities":—a king (who) thus discriminates among servants, is well-supplied with good servants.

Thus, also:—

74. A horse, a weapon, a book, a lute, speech, a man, and a woman, become useful or useless according to the peculiarities of the person who has obtained them.

Besides:—

75. What (benefit accrues) by one faithful, without ability? What, by one able (but) antagonistic? Me, both faithful and able, O king! thou shouldst not despise.

For:—

76. From the king's contempt, (his) retinue becomes devoid of understanding; therefore, from that principle, no sensible person is (likely to be) near. On the kingdom being deserted by the wise, the policy is not good; on the policy being weakened, the whole world necessarily sinks.

Moreover, Sire!—

77. Subjects always respect a man respected by the king; but he who (is) despised by the king, everybody despises.

Moreover:—

78. By wise people an appropriate observation is accepted even from a child. On the invisibility of the sun, is not the light of a lamp (availed of)?"

Tawny exclaimed: "Worthy Damanaka! how (is) this? Thou the intelligent son of our prime-minister, from some slanderous speech, hast passed all this time without coming near. Now speak as you please."

Damanaka boldly replied: "Sire! I ask you just to tell me,* why the master desirous of water, leaving the water undrunk, remained as if astonished?"

Tawny said: "Well spoken by thee; but we have no trustworthy person (for) this secret affair. Thou, indeed, (art) such a one; therefore, listen (and) I (will) relate (it):—This forest (is) now occupied by an extraordinary creature; hence (it) must be forsaken (by) us. And by thee, also, was heard likewise the unprecedented great noise. According to the noise, that creature must be (endued) with prodigious strength."

Damanaka remarked: "Sire! this is, to an extent, a great cause of fear. By us, also, the noise was heard; but is he a minister who, at first, without consultation, advises the king (to) abdicate (or) prepare for war? Besides, Sire! in this doubtful affair the utility of servants (is) to be ascertained. For:—

79. On the touchstone of misfortune a man ascertains the strength of the intellect

---

* *Lit.* "I am asking; let it just be said."

and goodness of the relation, wife, and servant class, and of himself."

Says the lion: "Friend, a great fear oppresses me." Damanaka said within himself: "Otherwise, how speak to me (of) abandoning the sweets of royalty to go to another place?" Aloud he says: "As long as I live, fear is not to be entertained. But let Karaṭaka and the rest be encouraged; whence (will arise) a hard-to-be-obtained body of men for the removal of the misfortune." Then both Damanaka and Karaṭaka, honoured with great favour by the king, having promised to counteract the danger, departed. (While) going along Karaṭaka said to Damanaka: "Friend! without knowing whether this cause of fear is capable of counteraction, or incapable of counteraction, how (is it that), promising the removal of the danger, this great favour has been accepted? For, without having done a service, a present should not be accepted from anyone; especially from a king. Observe:—

80. In whose favour prosperity is seated, in (whose) prowess is victory, and in (whose) anger resides death,—he surely (is) all-glorious.

Thus also:—
81. Although a child, a king is not to be despised, like an (ordinary) man; (for) a great divinity (is) this, residing in human form."

Says Damanaka laughingly: "Friend! remain silent; the cause of alarm is known by me (to be) the bellowing (of) a bull; and bulls (are) food for us; how much more so for a lion!"

Karaṭaka asked: "If so, then, why was not the master's fear removed on the spot?"

Damanaka replied: "If the master's fear had been removed on the spot, then how would there have been the acquisition of this great favour? Besides:—

82. A master should never be made free from solicitude by servants; a servant having made (his) master free from solicitude would be like Curd-ear."

Karaṭaka asked: "How (was) that?"

Damanaka relates (as follows):—There is, in northern parts, on a mountain named Million-peaked, a lion called Great-valour, the tip of whose mane, as he lay sleeping (in) the mountain cavern, a certain mouse (habitually) nibbles. The lion, perceiving the tip of his mane cut, was angry, (and) the mouse, (having) slipt into his hole, (and) being unattainable, he reflected (thus),—What (is) to be done here? Well, it is well known—

83. He of whom there should be an insignificant foe, (that foe) is not overcome by valour; to capture him a combatant like himself should be employed.

Having thus reflected, (and) gone to a village, (and) gratified with flesh and other kind of food, (and) with much pains brought (him), a cat named Curd-ear was placed by him in his cave. Then from fear of that (cat) the mouse did not come out. In consequence the lion slept tranquilly with his mane unclipped. Whenever he hears the noise of the mouse, then especially he pampers the cat with a gift of animal food. Now once the mouse pained by hunger, coming out, was caught by the cat, killed and eaten. Afterwards the lion heard no more the sound of the mouse; then, from want of (further) use, he became remiss in presenting the cat's food. Hence I say "(A master) should not be made free from solicitude," &c.

Then both Damanaka and Karaṭaka went near Lively. There Karaṭaka seated himself, with stateliness, at the foot of a tree, (and) Damanaka, going towards Lively, said : "Hulloh, bull-fellow, I (am) he appointed by King Tawny for the protection of the forest. General Karaṭaka orders (thus),—Come quickly ; if not, move off to a distance from this forest ; otherwise the consequences will be disagreeable to you. I know not what (my) angered master will do. For :—

84. For kings, the breach of commands ; for Brâhmans, disrespect ; for women, a separate bed,—(each is, as it were,) death without a weapon.

Then, ignorant of the customs of the country, Lively, having timidly advanced, profoundly saluted Karaṭaka. Thus it is said :—

85. " Reason, indeed, (is) stronger than force, for, in (its) absence, this (is) the condition of elephants ":—thus proclaims, as it were, the sounding drum of an elephant, struck by the elephant-driver.

Then Lively said with alarm.—General! let what (is) to be done by me be declared.

Karaṭaka replied : " Bull ! if there exists a wish to remain here in the forest, then go (and) salute the lotus-foot of the king."

Says Lively : " Then give a promise of safety, (and) I (will) go."

Karaṭaka said : " Listen, bull-fellow ! enough (of) this apprehension. For :—

86. Keśava* gave no reply to the King of Chedi (when) cursing ; for the maned (lion) roars responsive (to) the noise of the thunder-cloud, not (to) jackal-yells.

Besides :—

87. The tempest does not uproot tender grasses, (which) bend quite low. It throws down, indeed, lofty trees. The great expend valour only on the great.

Then they, having placed Lively at no great distance, went towards Tawny ; then, having been courteously regarded by the king, (they) saluted (him, and) sat down."

The king asked : " Was he seen ? "

Damanaka replied : " Sire ! (he) was seen. What was heard by the king, (is) indeed correct. He (is) very strong, (and) he wishes to see the king's foot.† Let the king be prepared (and) seated ; but, from a mere sound, (one) should not be afraid.

88. By water an embankment is broken ; so, also, (is) unkept counsel ; from backbiting friendship is broken ; a coward (is), indeed, to be broken by words.

Thus it has been said :—

89. Not knowing the cause of the noise, (one) should not be timid from a mere sound. Having ascertained the cause of a sound, a bawd attained respectability."

The king asked : " How (was) that ? "

Damanaka related (as follows) :—There is, in the midst of the Holy Mountains, a town called the City of Brahma. A popular rumour was current that there, on the mountain's top, a goblin named Bell-ear was dwelling. Once, having taken some-

---

* Krishna, the handsome-haired god (*kes'a* = hair). The allusion is to the capture of Rukmiṇî.
† i.e. to pay his respects to the king.

body's bell, while making off, a certain thief was killed by a tiger; the bell fallen from his hand was picked up by the monkeys; and those monkeys every minute were ringing that bell. Then it was perceived by the townspeople that a man had been devoured, and the noise of the bell is incessantly heard; thereupon the people declaring that Bell-ear, enraged, is devouring men and ringing the bell, all fled from the town. After (a time) the king was (thus) addressed by a procuress named Gaping, who, having reflected, had satisfied herself (that) monkeys were ringing the bell: "Sire! if a certain outlay of money be made then I (will) finish this Bell-ear." Then money was given to her by the delighted king. The procuress, having drawn a (magic) circle, and having shown homage to Ganeśa and other (gods), taking (with her) fruits liked by monkeys, entered the wood alone (and) scattered the fruit about. Then abandoning the bell, the monkeys were attracted (by) the fruit; and the procuress, picking up the bell, returned to the town (and) was honoured by all the people. Hence I say, "From a mere sound one should not be alarmed," &c.

Then having brought Lively, they effected an interview. Afterwards, he dwelt most affectionately for a long time there in the forest. Now once, the brother of the lion, named Stiff-ear, came (there). Having made him welcome, and seated (him), Tawny next sallied forth to kill beasts for a repast. Hereupon Lively said: "Sire! where (is) the flesh of the beasts killed to-day?" The king replied: "Damanaka and Karaṭaka know." Says Lively: "Let it be ascertained whether there is (any) or not." The lion laughingly said: "Then, there is none." Says Lively: "What! all that meat eaten by those two!" The lion said: "Eaten, given away, and wasted: this (is) the course daily." Lively says: "What! is this done without the knowledge of your highness?" The lion said: "Truly, it is done without my knowledge." Says Lively: "That is not proper. Thus it has been said:—

90. One should not, of himself, do any act for a master, without informing (him thereof),—other than the prevention of misfortune.

Besides:—

91. A minister, O king! (is) like an ascetic's gourd,—letting out little (and) taking in much. What's-a-moment (is) a blockhead; What's-a-cowrie (is) poor.*

92. He truly (is) always the best minister who increases (the revenue) by even one *kákini*.† The treasury (is) the life of a king possessed of a treasury; the vital airs (are) not the life.

93. Moreover, a man does not, by caste-observances, attain the state of being honoured by others: destitute of wealth he is deserted by his own wife; how much more by strangers!

And this (is) a grave fault in government. Observe:—

94. Extravagance and want of investigation, also unrighteous acquisition, (and) peculation by those residing at a distance (from the capital, are) called the bane of the treasury.

---

* *Kimkshaṇa* and *kimvarátaka* may be adjectives; thus, "Despising a moment (the minister is) a blockhead; despising a cowrie (he is) poor."
† Very small coin.

For :—

95. Even a rich man, equal to Ugly-ears,* inconsiderately spending (his) income according to his inclination, is speedily beggared."

Having heard that, Stiff-ear says: "Listen, brother! These two old dependants (are) the administrators of the affairs of peace and war; an administrator of the executive should not be appointed controller of the treasury. Moreover, on the subject of public functionaries, what little I have heard I (will) relate:

96. A Brâhman, a soldier, (or) a relative, is not commended in authority; a Brâhman does not give even the wealth provided (for the purpose), except reluctantly.

97. A soldier employed quickly shows the sword in a money matter; a relative, encroaching from relationship, swallows all the money.

98. A long-employed servant (is) fearless although in fault, and disregarding (his) master, he acts without restraint.

99. One who has done a service, (when) possessed of power, heeds not his own wrong-doing; making (his) service a banner, he plunders everything.

100. A minister jested with privately himself reigns unchecked; from familiarity contempt is always quickly shown by him.

101. One inwardly wicked, endued with patience, (is) assuredly the cause of every evil; S'akuni and S'akaṭâra† (are), in this matter, two illustrations.

102. Every minister to be appointed should never be wealthy. This (is) a maxim of the accomplished—Wealth (is) a perverter of the mind.

103. Not securing the advantage gained; the bartering of property; compliance; neglect; want of judgment; (and) pleasure; (are) the ruin of a minister.

104. To kings belong the expedient of seizing the wealth of officials; constant inspection; the gift of preferment; and also change of office.

105. Officials are generally like a hard tumour; unsqueezed they do not give forth the inner store of kings.

106. Officials, custodians of the king's treasure, are to be repeatedly cleared out. (Only) once squeezed, would a bathing-dress give out much water?

Knowing all this (the subject is) to be dealt with as occasion may require."

Says Tawny : " That is indeed so; but these in all respects do not execute my commands." Stiff-ear replies : " That is every way improper.

---

* *Vais'ravaṇa* (Ugly-oar) or *Kuvera* (Ugly-body), are names of the god of wealth.
† S'akuni, the counsellor of Duryodhana, who led the Pâṇḍava princes into gambling and the consequent loss of their possessions. S'akaṭâra, the minister of Nanda, who helped the Brâhman Châṇakya to put Chandragupta on the throne.

For :—

107. A king should not tolerate even (his) children breaking his commands; else what difference (is there) between a king and the picture of a king.

Besides :—

108. Of the stubborn, the glory perishes; of the inconstant, the friendship; of one deprived of sensual organs, the family (perishes); of one intent on wealth, the virtue; the fruit of knowledge, of the vicious; of a miser, the peace; of a king with a careless minister, the kingdom (perishes).

Especially :—

109. From thieves, from officials, from enemies, from the king's favourite, and from his own avarice, a king should protect (his) subjects, like a father.

Brother! by all means, let my advice be acted on. We have made our meal to-day; let this corn-eating Lively be appointed to the care of the food." On his suggestion being carried out, Tawny and Lively, giving up all (other) connections, are passing the time with great friendship. By and by, from perceiving a slackness in serving out the food of the dependants, Damanaka and Karaṭaka communed with each other. Then said Damanaka: "What (is) here to be done? This (is) a blunder committed by ourselves. On a fault being committed by oneself, grieving (is) improper. Thus it is said :—

110. I, having touched Gold-streak; and the messenger (who) bound herself; and the merchant who wished to take the jewel;—these from their own fault were pained.

Karaṭaka asks : " How (was) that?" Damanaka relates (as follows):—There is, in in a city named Golden-town, a king called Hero-valour. (While) his minister of justice was leading a certain barber (to) the place of execution, a wandering mendicant named Cupid's-banner, accompanied by a trader, held on to the skirt of (his) dress, exclaiming, "This one (is) not to be executed." The king's officers said : "Why (is) he not to be executed?" He said : "Let (this) be heard" : He (then) recites (the verse) " I having touched Gold-streak," &c. Said they : "What (is) that?" The mendicant relates (as follows) :—I (am) Cupid's-banner, the son of Cloud-banner, king of Ceylon. Now, once while in the pleasure-garden, from the mouth of a sea-faring merchant (it) was heard by me, that, in the midst of the sea (which was) near, on the fourteenth (day of the month), at the foot of an apparent Kalpa-tree,[*] seated on a couch variegated with radiant strings of jewels, adorned with every ornament, like Lakshmî,[†] playing the lute, a certain girl was to be seen. Then I, taking that sea-going merchant, having embarked (on board) a ship, went there. Thereupon (upon) going there she was seen by me exactly (as described) ; then, attracted by the nature of her beauty, a plunge was taken by me after (her). Immediately, having reached a golden city, in a palace of gold, attended upon by fairies in the bloom of youth, she was beheld by me, seated on a couch just (as described). Having seen (me) from a distance, she sent a friend, (and) I was courteously accosted. And then her friend, questioned by me, explained ;

---

[*] A tree of Paradise, fulfilling all wishes. [†] The goddess of prosperity, wife of Vishṇu.

"This, truly, is Jewel-stalk, daughter of Cupid-sport, emperor of the fairies. She has promised (thus): Whoever, having come, shall see the golden city with his own eyes, he, even in the absence of (my) father, shall marry me." Thereupon (I) married her with the Gandharva ceremony.* Then, on the Gandharva ceremony being completed, I remained sporting with her a long time. One day she said to me in private: "Husband, all this (is) to be freely enjoyed; but this depicted fairy named Gold-streak (is) never to be touched." Afterwards, through the curiosity (thus) engendered, that Gold-streak was touched by my hand; and, (for) acting thus, I was spurned by that picture with (its) lotus-foot, so that I alighted in the country of Surat. Since then, I, a wretched mendicant wandering the earth, have reached this city; and now, the day being far advanced, in a cowherd's house (I) slept, (and there) beheld (the following adventure):—In the evening, having entertained (his) friends, the cowherd returned from the pasture (and) saw his wife conversing with a procuress. Then, having beaten the cowherdess, (and) tied her hands to a post of the house, (he) went to sleep. In the middle of the night the messenger, this barber's wife, came again, (and) said to the cowherdess: "The worthy fellow, consumed by the fire of thy absence, is as though about to die; therefore, I, having bound myself, (will) remain here; do thou go, converse with him, (and) return quickly." On this being done, the cowherd waking, said: "Why now art thou not going to (thy) gallant?" When the procuress said nothing, then exclaiming, "From pride thou art giving no answer to my speech," the wicked fellow, through mistaking (her for) his wife, straightway cut off her nose. Having done so, the cowherd again laid down (and) went to sleep. Now having conversed with the gallant, the cowherdess returned, (and) quickly asked the procuress, close in (her) ear, "Goody, what news?" The procuress said: "Behold, my face indeed tells the news." The cowherdess, then, having bound herself just as before, stood (there); and the procuress, taking the severed nose, entered her own house, (and) remained (there). Early in the morning, the razor-case was asked for by this barber, to make his rounds in the town; she, not giving to him the razor-case, gave a single razor. Thereupon this barber, angry at not receiving the whole of the case, threw the razor from some distance at (his) wife. Then she, making cries of pain, (and) exclaiming, "Without any fault my nose has been cut by him," led him before the magistrate. (On the other hand) the cowherdess, on being questioned by the cowherd, said: "O wretch! who (is) able to disfigure me, most chaste? The eight guardian (deities) of the world are aware of my conduct. For:—

111. "Sun and moon, wind and fire, heaven, earth, the waters, the heart, and Yama,† day and night, both twilights, and justice, are cognizant of man's conduct.

"If, then, I should be perfectly chaste, (and) leaving thee, know not another, (and) not even in a dream have enjoyed another man, then let my face be uninjured." Accordingly, as soon as the cowherd brought a light (and) examines her face, at once, seeing the face with a prominent nose, (he) fell at her feet (and) having ardently em-

---

* That is, without any ceremony at all, *see* Manu iii. 32.   † The judge of the dead.

braced her, apologised. And as to this trader standing (here), listen also to his story. He started from his own house (and) after twelve years (he) came from the neighbourhood of Malaya to this city. Here he slept in a harlot's house. On the head of a demon carved out of wood, placed by the harlot at the house-door, is a valuable jewel. Perceiving that, this trader, greedy of gain, having risen in the night, to ascertain how much this valuable jewel might be worth, placed (his) hand on the gem, and pulled the jewel forcibly. Instantly being squeezed by the arms of the demon moved by wires, he roared with pain. Thereupon the harlot getting up said : " Son, thou art come from the neighbourhood of Malaya ; therefore, give up all (your) jewels, otherwise thou art not to be released by him. Just thus, this servant (always acts)." Then all (his) jewels were surrendered by him ; and now he, stripped of his all, is found among us (mendicants). Having heard all this, justice was administered by the king's officers. The barber's wife was shaved ; the cowherdess was banished ; the procuress was fined ; (and) the wealth of the trader was restored. Hence, I say, " I, having touched Gold-streak," &c. From this (it is evident that) this blunder was committed by ourselves. In this case regret (is) absurd. Having reflected a moment (Damanaka added), " Friend, as the friendship of these two was brought about hastily by me, so also is a separation to be effected. For :—

112. The dexterous make even untruths appear truths ; as people skilled in painting (can make) hollows and eminences on a level (surface).

Beside:—

113. On even the happening of emergencies he whose mind is not confused, gets quit of difficulties ; like the cowherdess (and) the pair of gallants.

Karaṭaka says : " How (is) that ? " Damanaka relates (as follows) :—There is, in the city (named) Many-gated, an unchaste woman the wife of a certain cowherd ; and she amuses herself with the magistrate of the village and his son. Thus it is said :—

114. Fire is not satisfied with wood ; nor the ocean with rivers ; nor Death with all creatures, nor bright-eyed women with men.

Again :—

115. Not by liberality, nor by honour, nor by rectitude, nor by homage, nor by punishment, nor by precept (can they be made faithful) : women (are) altogether bad.

For :—

116. Women, abandoning a husband, virtuous, famous, handsome, skilled in love, wealthy, and young ; straightway betake themselves to a man destitute of amiability, merit, and so forth.

Moreover :—

117. A woman does not experience such satisfaction, even sleeping at ease on an embroidered bed, as the pleasure she attains from the companionship of a strange lover, on the (mere) ground strewed with durva grass, and the like.

Now she, on an occasion, was sitting sporting with the son of the magistrate ; thereupon the magistrate also arrived. Perceiving him, having placed his son in a store-room, she played in the same manner with the magistrate. In the meantime, ner husband the cowherd returned from the pasture. Seeing him, the cowherdess said: "Magistrate, having taken thy stick, seeming to be angry, hastily go." On this being done, the cowherd coming there questioned (his) wife: "Through what business came the magistrate here?" Says she: "He, for some reason or other, is angered with his son, and (the son) being pursued, came here and entered through fear. Putting (him) into the store-room, he was saved by me; and (he) was (therefore) not seen in the house by his father seeking (for him); hence the latter is going away angry." Then, having brought the son down from the store-room she showed (him). Thus it is said:—

118. The food of women is known (to be) two-fold; their wit four-fold; (their) ingenuity six-fold; and (their) lust eight-fold.

Hence I say, "Even upon the occurrence of emergencies," &c.

Karaṭaka said: "Be that as it may; but how can their great natural affection be severed?" Damanaka replied: "A stratagem (is) to be devised. Thus it is said:—

119. What is possible by a stratagem, is not possible by valorous deeds. A she-crow caused a black snake to be killed by a gold chain."

Karaṭaka asked: "How (was) that?" Damanaka related (thus):—In a certain tree dwell a pair of crows; and their young were devoured by a black snake living in a hollow of the tree. Then, breeding again, the she-crow says: "Husband, this tree should be abandoned; as long as the black snake (is) here, so long will there never be offspring. For:—

120. A wicked wife, a false friend, a servant giving (saucy) answers, and residence in a house with a snake (in it, is) death, without doubt.

Says the crow: "Beloved, (it is) not to be feared; repeatedly his great offence has been borne by me; now (it is) not to be again endured." The she-crow said: "How (is) your honour able to contend with this powerful black snake?" Says the crow: "Enough (of) this anxiety. For:—

121. He who (has) intelligence (has) strength; whence (comes) the strength of the senseless? Behold! the lion intoxicated by pride, was overthrown by a hare.

The she-crow said: "How (was) that?" The crow relates (as follows): There is, on the mountain called Bulky, a lion named Hard-to-tame; and he is constantly engaged in the slaughter of beasts. Then the lion was (thus) addressed by all the beasts assembled together: "Sire, for what purpose is a slaughter of all the beasts made at once? Truly we, for your honour's food, every day (will) present a beast." The lion said: "If that (is) the desire of your honours, then let it be so." Now all by regular succession, each day are giving a beast; (and) thenceforward, every day he is accustomed to eat, one by one, the beast allotted. Now, on a certain day, the turn of an old hare (being) come, he reflected (thus):—

122. Because of fear, homage is rendered, (in) hope of life; if I must go to destruction, what (advantage will result) to me by civility to the lion?

Therefore I (will) approach very leisurely. Then the lion, pressed by hunger, angrily said to him: "Wherefore art thou come tardily?" The hare said: "I (am) not faulty; on the way (I was) forcibly detained by another lion. Having sworn to come again before him, I am come here to inform (my) master." The lion angrily said: "Go quickly; show me, where is this villain?" Then the hare, having taken him, came close to a deep well. Having said, "Let (my) master come here (and) see," he showed (him) his own reflection in the water of that well. Then he, inflated with anger, from pride casting himself upon that (reflected image), attained destruction. Hence I say, "He who (has) intelligence," &c. Says the she-crow: "(What you have been saying has been) heard by me, say (what is) to be done." The crow said: "My dear, the king's son comes constantly (and) bathes in the adjacent pool. Having seized and conveyed with (thy) beak the gold chain taken from his body (and laid) on that stone thou wilt place (it) in this hollow." Now, on a certain day, as soon as the king's son, having placed the gold chain on a stone, had entered (the water) to bathe, that (plan) was executed by the she-crow. Then the black snake being discovered by the king's officers engaged in searching for the gold chain, was put to death. Hence I say, "What is possible by a stratagem," &c.

Karaṭaka (then) said: "If so, then go. May the paths be prosperous to you!" Then Damanaka, having approached Tawny, said respectfully: "Sire, thinking over a certain urgent and most alarming affair, I am come to impart (it). For:—

123. In (case of) misfortune, in going on a wrong course, and on the opportunities for (efficacious) action passing away; a friendly man, even unasked, should utter useful advice.

Besides:—

124. The king (is) a vessel of enjoyment; the minister a vessel of work: from failure of the king's affairs the minister incurs blame.

This (is) the (proper) course for ministers—

125. Better resigning life,* or even decapitation, but not the tolerance of one meditating the crime of usurping the dignity of (his) master.

Tawny respectfully says: "Now what does your honour desire to say?" Damanaka said: "This much: Lively manifests improper behaviour towards thee; and also, in my presence, having despised the master's triple power,† even lusts for sovereignty." Having heard this, Tawny stood mute with fear (and) astonishment. Damanaka continued: "Sire, having discarded every (other) minster this one has been appointed to the superintendence of all affairs by thee. And this (is) a grave error. For:—

---

* Euphemism for "suicide."
† 1. *prabhutwa*, the majesty of the king; 2. *mantra*, the force of good counsel; 3. *utsâha*, the force of energy.

126. When a minister and a king is (each) excessively exalted, Prosperity, having fixed both (her) feet, stands (firmly); she, from (her) female nature, impatient of the weight of both (at once), abandons one or the other of the two.

Again :—
127. When a king makes one sole minister in the kingdom, from infatuation pride approaches him, and he is estranged by the indolence of pride; in the heart of the estranged, a hankering for independence makes a foot-hold; thence, through a desire for independence, he plots the death of the king.

And it is said :—
128. The complete removal* of poisoned food, a loose tooth, and a wicked minister (gives) ease.

Moreover :—
129. The king who makes prosperity dependent on a minister, he, on the happening of calamity sinks, like the blind without guides.

And he acts in all affairs according to his own inclination. Here, your Majesty (is) the authority.† But this I know from experience,
130. There is not the man in the world, who does not desire fortune. Who does not look wishfully at another's charming young (wife)?"

The lion, having reflected, said : "Friend, although (that is) so, still my friendship with Lively (is) great. Observe :—
131. Although committing faults, he who (is) beloved is indeed beloved; (to) whom (is) the body not dear, although defiled by endless imperfections.

Besides :—
132. Although doing unfriendly (acts), he who (is) beloved, is indeed beloved; on even the finest house being burned, who (feels) disrespect (for) fire?"

Says Damanaka : "Sire! that (is) indeed a fault. For :—
133. On whom the king much casts an eye, on a son, a minister, or on a stranger, that person is courted by Fortune. Mark this, Sire!

134. The end of what is salutary, although unpleasant, brings happiness; where there is both a speaker and a listener, there successes disport (themselves).

But, having cast aside hereditary servants, this stranger has been advanced by thee; and this was improperly done. For :—
135. Through the fault of hereditary servants (a king) should not cherish strangers; there is no other greater cause of dissension in a kingdom than this."

Says the lion : "Mighty strange! since, after giving an assurance of safety, he has been brought and promoted by me, how, then, is he plotting?"
Damanaka replied : "Sire!
136. A bad person reverts (to his) natural character even (while) being assiduously

---

* *Lit.* "tearing up from the root."
† That is, "your inclination, not his, should be the guiding principle."

well treated : as a dog's tail, with* (all) expedients of warming and anointing (remains) bent.

Again :—

137. Warmed, pressed, and even swathed with bandages, (when) liberated, after a dozen years, a dog's tail resumed (its) natural character.

Again :—

138. How (can) the promotion and honour of the vile (conduce) to conciliation ? poison-trees, though watered with nectar, do not bear wholesome fruits.

Hence I say :

139. Even unasked (a man) should utter what is friendly for one whose ruin he may not desire; this, indeed, (is) the law of the good; the reverse of it (that) of the wicked.

And it is said :—

140. He (is) kind who shields from harm; that (is) a (real) action which (is) pure; she (is) a wife who (is) obedient; he (is) wise who is honoured by the good; that (is) prosperity which does not cause pride ; he (is) happy who (is) free from hankering ; he (is) a friend who (is) inartificial; he (is) a man who is not tormented by (his) passions.

If the master, injured by the wickedness of Lively, although warned, does not desist, then (it is) no fault of the servant. Also :—

141. A king devoted to pleasure values neither duty nor interest; he rambles as he pleases, following his own inclinations, like an infuriated elephant. At length, when puffed up by pride he falls into an abyss of distress, then he casts the blame on the servant, and perceives not his own indiscretion."

Tawny (*aside*).

142. (A king) should not inflict punishment upon others through the accusation of another; after personal investigation, he should imprison or honour.

Thus it is said :—

143. (The distribution of) favour and punishment (when) not having considered in due form merit and blame (tends) to one's own destruction ; as (when) the hand from conceit is placed on the mouth of a serpent.

(*Aloud*).—" Then should Lively be admonished ? "

Damanaka (*hastily*).—" Not so, on any account. A breach of counsel is (in that way) produced. And it is said thus :—

144. This seed of counsel should be so preserved as that it should not be ever so little broken ; (when) it is broken it grows not.

Moreover :—

145. Time drinks up the flavour of what ought to be received, to be given, or of an act to be done, (when it is) not being done speedily.

Then, surely, what has been commenced, with great diligence should be completed.

Moreover :—

146. Counsel, like a wavering soldier, even with all (his) limbs covered, cannot bear to remain long, through fear of injury from the enemy.

---

* The instrumental case here has the sense " in despite of."

If he, detected in a fault, having turned from the fault (is) to be re-instated, that (is) exceedingly improper. For:—

147. He who wishes to re-establish a friend who has once offended, receives death; like a she-mule a fœtus."*

Says the lion: "Let it be known, at all events, what he (is) able to do against us." Damanaka replied: "Sire!

148. The nature of the body and its connections being unknown, how (can there be) a demonstration of ability? Behold! the sea was confounded by a mere sandpiper."

The lion asked: "How (was) that?" Damanaka related (as follows):—On the shore of the sea, a pair of sandpipers are dwelling. Now the hen, being about to lay, said (to her) husband: "Master! let a place suitable for laying be sought for." The sandpiper said: "Is not this very place suitable for laying?" Says she: "This place is overflowed by the waves of the sea." He replies: "My dear! am I without resource (that) eggs deposited in my house are carried away by the sea?" The hen smiling said: "Master! between thee and the sea the difference (is) great. Now:—

149. "(Am I) myself able to mitigate (this) misfortune, or not?"—of whom there is such discrimination, he sinks not even in a difficulty.

Also:—

150. The commencement of an improper act, opposition to one's own folk, rivalry with the stronger, (and) confidence in womankind, (are) the four gates of death.

Then, by direction of her mate, she laid (in) that very place. Having heard all this (and) intent on knowing his strength, his eggs were removed by the sea. Then the hen, afflicted with grief, said (to her) husband: "Master! a misfortune has happened, my eggs are lost." The sandpiper replied: "My dear! fear not." Having said this (and) having convened an assembly of the birds, (he) went (to) the presence of Garuḍa, lord of winged creatures; (there) he relates the tale of the destruction of his eggs. Then, having heard his statement, the revered lord Nârâyaṇa, cause of creation, preservation, and destruction, was informed (thereof) by that winged-one. Thereupon, obeying† the Lord's command, he went to the sea, (and) the sea, having heard his command, surrendered those eggs. Hence I say, "Without knowing the nature of the body and its connections," &c.

The king asked: "How (is) he to be known as treacherous?" Damanaka replied: "When he comes prepared to strike with the points of (his) horns, as if apprehensive, then the master will know."

Having spoken thus, (he) went towards Lively; and being gone there, slowly drawing near, made himself appear as though amazed. Then said Lively courteously: "Friend Damanaka! prosperity to thee!" Damanaka replies: "Whence (comes) the prosperity of dependants? For:—

151. Their successes (are) subject to others, (with) mind ever unquiet, even uncertain in (regard to) their own life, (such are) they who depend on kings.

---

* Referring to the notion that gestation kills a mule.
† Lit. "having placed the lord's command on his head."

Again :—

152. Who having acquired riches (is) not proud? Of what wordling (are) the troubles gone to their setting? Of whom upon the earth (is) not the mind distressed by women? Who, indeed, (is) beloved (by) kings? Who has not gone into the arms of death? What supplicator has attained dignity? Or what man, fallen into the toils of the wicked, has escaped with safety?

Lively said : "Friend, tell (me); what (is) this?"

Damanaka replied: "What (shall) I say, unhappy wretch (that I am)! See :—

153. As (when) sunk in the ocean, (and) having obtained the support of a serpent, one neither lets go nor retains hold, so now am I perplexed.

For :—

154. On the one hand, the king's confidence is lost; on the other hand, a friend. What (shall) I do, where (shall) I go, fallen into a sea of trouble!"

Having said this, sighing deeply, (he) sat down.

Lively (then) says: "Nevertheless, friend, let what is passing in the mind be related in detail."

Damanaka said whisperingly : "Although the king's confidence must not be divulged to another, still your honour, through my promise, came and remained, therefore, (what concerns) thy welfare should be imparted by me, desirous of the next world. Listen. This master estranged from thee* declared privately—Having killed Lively, I (will) satisfy my retinue.

Hearing this Lively became exceedingly dejected.

Damanaka continued: "Enough of dejection! let an action appropriate to the time be adopted."

Lively, reflecting awhile, said : "This, indeed, is plainly declared :—

155. Women (are) accessible to the wicked ; the king is often a supporter of the unworthy; wealth (is) an attendant on the niggardly; Deva† rains upon rock and sea.

Also :—

156. Lakshmi‡ consorts with the base; Saraswatî,§ with the plebeian; a woman courts the unworthy; Vâsava‖ rains on a mountain.

(Aside).—Whether this (be) his doing or not, cannot be ascertained from his behaviour. For :—

157. Any bad person acquires lustre from the beauty of (his) patron; like smutty collyrium applied to the eye of a lovely woman.

Then having reflected, (he) exclaimed: Alas! what (is) this that has happened? For :—

158. A king being served assiduously does not attain satisfaction : (have we) here a wonder? But this (is) an unprecedented kind of object, who, being served, (actually) attains enmity.

Here, then, diligence (is) unavailing. For :—

159. He who is angry for a cause, on the removal of that (cause) is speedily tranquillized ; but how, forsooth, shall a man satisfy him whose mind is inimical without cause?

---

* *Lit.* Upon thee.   † A name of Indra, the giver of rain.   ‡ The goddess of prosperity.
§ The goddess of eloquence.   ‖ A name of Indra.

What has been done by me against the king? or (are) kings causelessly injurious? Damanaka said: "It (is) even so. Listen:—

160. Even a service (performed) by the discreet (and) affectionate incurs odiousness, whilst an injury (done) by others openly finds favour. How surprising, then, is the conduct of those who resort to the fickle! The pre-eminently difficult duty of service (is) unattainable even (to) Yogins.

Moreover:—
161. A hundred acts (of kindness are) lost upon the wicked: a hundred fine speeches (are) lost upon the stupid: a hundred maxims (are lost) upon the disregarder of advice: a hundred (wise) thoughts (are) lost upon the thoughtless.

Again:—
162. In sandal-trees (there are) serpents. In the waters, lotuses; but there are (also) alligators. Spiteful detractors (are) in (our) enjoyment. (There are) no unobstructed pleasures.

Again:—
163. The root (swarms) with serpents; the blossoms with bees; the branches with monkeys; the upper parts with bears. There is not, truly, that (part) of a sandal-tree which (is) not infested by the vilest impurities.

That this (our) master, says Damanaka, (is) honey-spoken (and) poison-hearted is known by me. For:—
164. The hand outstretched from afar—the eye suffused—half the seat relinquished—intent on a close embrace—respectful in kind conversation (and) inquiries—concealed poison within, honied without—beyond measure an adept in deceit;—what a wondrous art of mimicry truly (is) this, learned by the wicked!

In like manner:—
165. A boat (is the expedient) in traversing a mass of water difficult to cross; a lamp (is the expedient) on the approach of darkness; in a calm, a fan; a hook, for curbing the fury of an elephant blind with passion. Thus there is nothing upon earth for which the thought of an expedient has not been taken by the Creator: I think (that) even the Creater (is) baffled in removing the inward purpose of the wicked."

Lively (said) to himself: O misery! how (is it that) I, a corn-eater (am) to be slain by the lion? For:—
166. Truly between two equal (in) wealth, (and) between two equal (in) strength, a controversy may be imagined; (but) nowhere between two, (one) high (the other) low.

Having reflected again, he said: "By whom has this king been made to change towards me? From a king close upon a rupture, fear (is) ever to be entertained. For:—
167. (If) the mind of the king (is) anywhere severed, like a bracelet of crystal, who (is) the master to join (it) together?

Again:—
168. A thunderbolt and the king's severity, (are) both exceedingly terrible: one falls on a single spot, the other falls all around.

Therefore let death in battle be resorted to; now obedience to his command (would be) improper. For:—

169. Either (by) dying he obtains heaven, or having slain the enemy (he obtains) pleasures; both these excellencies, very difficult of acquisition (are the prerogatives) of heroes.

And this (is) the time for war:—

170. Where (in) peace (there is) certain destruction (and) in war a chance of life, that, truly, the wise declare the time for war.

For:—

171. When in peace he should perceive nothing beneficial (to) himself; then the wise man dies combatting with the enemy.

172. In victory one obtains prosperity, also by dying (one obtains) a celestial bride; bodies perish in a moment; what anxiety (need there be) about dying in battle.

Having reflected thus Lively said: "O friend, how (is it) to be ascertained that he (is) desirous to slay me?" Says Damanaka: "When he looks at thee (with) ears erect, tail elevated, claws raised, (and) gaping mouth, then wilt thou likewise display thy bravery. For:—

173. Of whom (is) not one destitute of energy, although strong, an object of humiliation? Observe, the foot is fearlessly placed by people on a heap of ashes.

But all this (is) to be accomplished very secretly; otherwise, neither thou nor I (will prosper)." Saying this Damanaka went to Karaṭaka. Karaṭaka said: "What (is) the result?" Damanaka replied: "The result (is) mutual estrangement between them." Karaṭaka rejoined: "What doubt (can there be) here? For:—

174. Who, indeed, (is) a friend of the wicked? Who, excessively importuned, is not angered? Who is not rendered arrogant by wealth? Who (is) not an adept in villainy?

Again:—

175. An illustrious (person) is made infamous by rogues for their own advantage. Does not, indeed, association with the vile act like fire?

Then Damanaka having approached Tawny (said): "Sire! that evil-intentioned (one) is come, therefore stand prepared." Having said which, he caused him to assume the appearance stated above. Lively, also, having approached, (and) seeing the lion in that way altered in appearance, showed fight after his own fashion. Then in the great conflict between them Lively was killed by the lion. Now the lion having killed (his) servant Lively sat resting sorrowfully, and he says: What a cruel deed has been committed by me! For:—

176. By others is the kingdom enjoyed; he himself (is) a vessel of iniquity. By outraging duty a king is like a lion after the slaughter of an elephant.*

Besides:—

177. In (estimating) the loss of a portion of territory, or of a virtuous (and) wise minister, the loss of a minister (is) the death of kings.

---

* Because others appropriate the pearls said to be in the head of the dead elephant.

SUHRIDBHEDA.

Damanaka said: "O master! what novel philosophy (is) this, that remorse is experienced after slaying an enemy! Thus, indeed, it has been said:—

178. If either father or brother, if either son or friend, (be) conspirators against (his) life, (they) should be killed by a king desiring prosperity.

Moreover:—

179. (One) knowing the principles of duty, interest, and pleasure, cannot be purely compassionate: a forbearing (person is) not able to preserve even the property (already) in his grasp.

Besides:—

180. Forbearance towards both an enemy and a friend (is), of a truth, the ornament of ascetics; (but) towards offending beings it (is), verily, for kings, a defect.

Furthermore:—

181. For (one) desiring his master's dignity, through lust of dominion (or) through conceit, forfeiture of life (is) the sole expiation; (there is) no other.

Again:—

182. A compassionate king, a Brahman (who) eats everything, a disobedient wife, an ill-natured friend, a refractory servant, an imprudent officer, and one who does not acknowledge what has been done,* these (are) to be avoided.

And especially:—

183. The policy of a king, like a courtezan, (is) many-shaped: true and false, harsh and kind-spoken, cruel and merciful, parsimonious and generous, ever spending yet (intent on) the influx of hoards of jewels and money."

Thus with deceitful speech tranquillised by Damanaka, Tawny regained his natural temper (and) sat on (his) throne. Damanaka being overjoyed in heart, said to the king: "May the monarch be victorious! may the whole world be prosperous!" Having said this he continued at ease.

Vishnuśarman said: "(You) have heard the Separation of Friends." The princes replied: "We (are) gratified." Vishnuśarman said: In future let this also be,—

184. May the separation of friends be (found) only in the abode of your Honour's enemies! May the wretch, drawn by Fate, day by day approach destruction! May mankind ever be the abode of all happiness and prosperity! May (every) boy also continually delight here in the charming garden of fable!

Here ends the Second Chapter of the Hitopadeśa, called the Separation of Friends.

---

* The ungrateful one.

WAR.

At the time for re-commencing the story the princes said: "Sir! we (are) princes; therefore, there is curiosity among us to hear (about) war." Vishnuśarman replied:— I discourse (about) that which is agreeable to your Highnesses. Attend to War, of which this is the first verse:—

1. In a war, equal in valour, of peacocks with geese, the geese, having been induced to confide, were deceived by crows (who) had lived in the enemy's town.

The princes asked: "How (was) that?" Vishnuśarman related (as follows):— There is, in the island of Camphor, a lake named Lotus-sport. There a flamingo dwells named Gold-egg; and he was inaugurated in the sovereignty of the birds by all the aquatic fowls assembled together. For:—

2. If there be no king, wholly a leader, then the subjects would be tossed about like a ship on the sea without a steersman.

Again:—

3. The king protects the subject; the subject aggrandizes the king: protection is better than aggrandizement; in its absence, even that which (is) existent, (is) non-existent.

Once upon a time this flamingo was sitting comfortably on a well-spread lotus-bed, his retinue standing around. Thereupon a crane named Long-face, coming from some country or other, having made obeisance, sat down. The king said: "Long-face! thou art come from a foreign land, relate the news." He replied: "Sire! there is important news; in (my) desire to tell it, I am come hastily. Let attention be paid. There is in Jambudwîpa a mountain named Vindhya, (and) there dwells a peacock named Spotted-colour, king of the birds. In the midst of a parched wood while pecking (food) I was seen and questioned by his attendants (thus): "Who (art) thou? whence (art) thou come?" Then I replied: "I (am) an attendant of Gold-egg, king of the island of Camphor; from curiosity I am come to see a foreign country." Having heard that the birds said: "Of the two, then, which country or king (is) the better?" Thereupon I replied: "Ah! what (is this which) is said! Great (is) the difference! for the island of Camphor is a district of heaven, and the king (is) a second lord of Paradise. How can it be described? What are you doing here, alighted in a barren place? Come, let (us) go into my country." Then, having heard that speech, the birds became angry.

As it is said:—

4. Milk-drinking (is) for serpents only the increase of venom. Advice (leads) to the exasperation, not to the tranquillization, of fools.

Again:—

5. A sensible (person) may be advised, but a blockhead, never. Birds having advised (certain) stupid monkeys, experienced the destruction of (their) homes.

The king asked: "How (was) that?" Long-face related (the following anecdote):—There is on the banks of the Narmadâ, in the land skirting the hills, a large silk-cotton tree. There, in a nest constructed by themselves (some) birds are residing comfortably, even during the rains. Now, on the nether sky being overspread with masses of cloud, like sheets of indigo, there was a great rain in torrents. Then, perceiving the monkeys standing under the tree, pinched with cold, (and) shivering, the birds compassionately said: "Ho, monkeys! hearken:

6. Nests have been built by us with straws brought with (our) beaks merely; how (is it that) you, endowed with hands, feet, &c., are dejected?"

Hearing this, the monkeys with (their) anger aroused, looked up, (and cried): "Oh! the comfortable birds, seated in the bosom of nests sheltered from wind, are taunting us. Let it be so, until an abatement of the rain." Afterwards, when the downpour of water had abated, the monkeys, having climbed the trees, broke all the nests, and threw down all the eggs of those birds. Hence I say, "A sensible (person) may be advised," &c. The king said: "What was said then by the birds?" Long-face resumed:—Then the birds angrily exclaimed, "By whom was this flamingo made king?" Then I with anger aroused, said: "By whom was this peacock of yours made king?" Upon hearing that the birds prepared to kill me; whereupon I also made a goodly display of valour. For:—

7. At another time, forbearance (is) the ornament of a man, as modesty (is) of a woman. At an insult, valour (is appropriate), as (is) lasciviousness in sexual embraces.

The king, laughing, said:—

8. He who, having investigated the strength and weakness of himself and others does not perceive the difference, he is scorned by the enemy.

Again:—

9. Grazing constantly for a very long time (on) the corn in a field, a stupid ass, covered in a tiger's skin, was killed, through the blunder of speaking.

The crane asked: "How (is) that?" The king related (as follows):—There was in Hastinâpura a washerman named Frolic. His donkey, from conveying excessive loads, was become weak (and) ready to die. Then the washerman, having clothed (him) in a tiger's skin, turned him loose in a field of corn in the vicinity of a forest. Then seeing him from afar, the owners of the field fled hastily away, with the idea (that it was) a tiger. Now a certain watcher of the corn, with a body-covering made of grey blanket, having prepared (his) bow and arrow, remained, in a crouching position, in a retired spot. Then seeing him at a distance, the donkey (with) recruited vigour, thinking him a female ass, trotted up to him braying. Thereupon he was killed, through (his) gamesomeness, by that cornwatcher, (when he) ascertained that it was (but) an ass. Hence I say that "For a very long time continuously grazing," &c. Long-face (then) resumed :—Afterwards those birds exclaimed, "O wicked, vile crane! (while) feeding on our ground thou art reviling our sovereign; that (is) not now to be endured." Saying which, all, striking me with (their) beaks angrily exclaimed: "See, O fool! this gander thy king (is) altogether spiritless: sovereignty is not his; for one gentle to an extreme (is) unable to retain the wealth already in his hand; how is he (then) ruling the earth? or what kingdom (is) his? But thou (art) a frog in a well, therefore thou advisest resort to him. Listen :—

10. A great tree having fruit and shade (is) to be respected: if, through fate, there be no fruit, by what (cause) is the shade withheld?

Again :—

11. The service of the base (is) not to be engaged in: resort (is) to be made to the great. Even water, in the hand of a tavern-keeper, is thought (to be) spirit.

12. The she-goat, by favour of the lion, browses fearlessly in the wood. Vibhîshaṇa, having met Râma, obtained sovereignty in Lankâ.*

Again :—

13. The great (possessed of) abundant virtues attain littleness, when (depending) on the worthless, through the relation of the receptacle and the object to be received; like an elephant in a (convex) mirror.

And especially :—

14. Even in a stratagem there may be success over an exceedingly powerful king. By the stratagem of the Moon, the hares dwell happily."

I asked : "How (is) that?" The birds related (this anecdote) :—Once upon a time, from the absence of rain even in the rainy season, a herd of elephants, troubled by thirst, said to the leader of the herd : "Sir, there is no means for our living. (There are) bathing-places for the lesser animals, but we, from the absence of bathing, (are) like the blind, (crying) Where are we going? What are we doing?" Then the elephant-king, having gone no great distance, pointed out a limpid pool. Soon after the hares dwelling on its banks (are) crushed by blows from the feet of the herd of elephants. Thereupon a hare named Blockhead reflected (thus) : "This herd of thirst-afflicted elephants will come here daily; hence our family (will be) destroyed." Then an old buck named Victory said : "Be not dejected, a remedy (can) be devised by me." Having thus promised (he) set out. Whilst going on (his) way he reflected (thus) : "Having approached the leader of the herd of elephants, what (is) to be said by me? For :—

15. Even (when) touching, an elephant kills; a serpent (when) smelling; a king, even (when) protecting; the wicked, even (when) smiling.

Therefore having mounted to the summit of a hill, I (will) address the elephant-leader." On this being done, the leader of the troop exclaimed: "Who (art) thou?

---

* Vibhîshaṇa was a brother of Râvana, who disapproving of his brother's wickedness, ultimately deserted his cause, and joining Râma, was placed by him upon the throne of Lankâ or Ceylon.

(and) whence come?" He replied: "I (am) a messenger sent by the revered Moon." The master of the herd rejoined: "Let (thy) business be declared." Victory said:—

16. "Even among uplifted weapons an envoy speaks not otherwise (than his errand); through his inviolable character (he is) always a speaker of the truth.

Therefore, I speak by his command; listen: Whereas these hares, guardians of the Moon's lake, have been driven away by thee,—that was not rightly done; for these protectors, the hares, (are) mine; for this (reason) my (title) Hare-marked (is) well-known." As soon as the messenger had spoken thus, the leader of the herd timidly said this: "Sire, this was done ignorantly; I will not go again." The messenger remarked: "Then, having here saluted and propitiated the revered Moon trembling with anger on the lake, do thou depart." Then having conducted (him) at night, and pointed out the reflection of the Moon quivering in the water, he caused the leader of the herd to salute it. "Sire, the fault was committed by him through ignorance, therefore, let it be forgiven," having said which the leader of the herd was dismissed by the hare. Hence I say, "There may be success even by a stratagem," &c. After that I said: "Truly he our sovereign (is) most mighty and exceedingly powerful, the sovereignty of the three worlds is appropriate to him; what, then, (is) a kingdom!" Then I was led into the presence of king Spotted-colour by those birds, (they) crying out, "Wretch! how art thou at large in our territory!" Then having exhibited me before the king, after salutation, they said: "Sire! let attention be paid. This vile crane, even while travelling in our country, despises the royal feet." The king inquired: "Who (is) this? whence has (he) come?" They replied: "He (is) a follower of the flamingo named Gold-egg; (and) is come from the island of Camphor. Then I was asked by the prime-minister, a vulture: "Who (is) there the prime-minister?" I replied: "A ruddy-goose named Know-all, thoroughly versed in all the sciences." Says the vulture: "That is right; he (is) a fellow-countryman. For:—

17. A fellow-countryman perfect in family observances, free from deceit, familiar with the sciences, not attached to wicked inclinations, devoid of immorality,—

18. Well read in the body of laws, renowned, of pure blood, prudent, a producer of wealth; a king may properly appoint (such a one as his) minister.

Thereupon a parrot, the superintendent of justice, said: "The island of Camphor, and the rest, (are) insignificant isles lying within Jambudwîpa; there also the sovereignty of the royal feet (extends)." Then the king also said: "Truly (that is) so." For:—

19. A king, a madman, a child, a wanton, and a purse-proud (man), hanker after even the unattainable; how much more (after) what is procurable!

Then I said: "If, by mere talk, the authority of your Majesty's feet is established, then the sovereignty of my lord Gold-egg also exists in Jambudwîpa." The parrot asked: "What demonstration (is there) in this case?" I replied: "Even war." The king jestingly remarked: "Go to your king, and make ready." Then said I: "Let your own envoy also be sent." The king remarked : "Who is to set out with the message*; for a messenger of this sort should be appointed—

20. An envoy should be loyal, talented, pure, dexterous, brave, virtuous, patient, a Brahman, conversant with the weak points of others, endowed with presence of mind."

Says the vulture : " There are many such ; still a Brahman should be made envoy. For :—

21. Perspicuity effects the success of a king, not nobility. From association with Iśwara, the blackness of kâlakûṭa† does not depart."

The king said : "Then let the parrot go. Parrot! do thou, going with him, declare our will." The parrot replied : " As your Majesty commands. But this (is) a wicked crane ; (and) along with a wicked person I travel not. Thus it has been said :—

22. A vile person does a bad action ; surely (that bad action) produces its effects among the good. Should the ten-headed one‡ carry off Sîtâ there would be a bridging§ of the ocean. Besides :—

23. One should not stand, equally one should not go, with a wicked person anywhere. From association with a crow, a gander was killed standing, and a quail going.

The king asked : "How (is) that?" The parrot (then) related :—There is, on the road to Ujjain, in a lonely path, a great peepul-tree, whereon a gander and a crow are dwelling. Once (upon a time), in the hot season, a certain wearied traveller, having placed his bow and arrows under a tree, dropt asleep there. Then, after a little while, the shade of the tree passed away from off his face. Thereupon, perceiving his face overspread by the glare of the sun, through pity, the charitable-souled, inoffensive gander, perched in the peepul-tree, having spread out (his) wings, again caused a shade (to fall) upon his face. Afterwards, (while) enjoying sound sleep, the wearied traveller, fatigued by travelling along the road, opened (his) mouth. Hereupon, through natural malevolence, unable to endure the comfort of others, the crow, having voided excrement into his mouth, flew away. Then, (the traveller) having arisen, looked up, (and) immediately the gander is perceived by him. Now, through the anger generated by thinking that the voidance of excrement into his mouth (was done) by this (gander), (he) having pierced (him) with an arrow, killed (him). Hence I say, " Not to be stood with," &c. For :—

24. Quit the society of the evil. Cultivate the society of the good. Practise virtue day and night. Remember always (your) transitoriness.

Sire ! I am (about to) relate also the story of the quail. A crow is lodging on the branch of a tree ; and a quail dwells on the ground beneath. Once upon a time, all the birds, by engaging in a pilgrimage (in honour) of the Worshipful Garuḍa,|| set off (towards) the sea-shore. Thither the quail went with the crow. Now from a pail, resting on the head of a dairyman going along on the road, (some) curds were again and again pecked by the crow. Then as soon as he, having placed the pail of curds on

---

* Interrogative with imperative ; *lit.* " Let whom go forth with the message ? "

† The name of a poison. In allusion to the blue neck of S'iva caused by swallowing the poison produced by the churning of the ocean by the gods and demons.

‡ An epithet of Râvaṇa, *see* Vishṇu-Purâṇa, Bk. iv. chap. iv.

§ The word *bandhanam* here means the " uniting " or " binding " of southern India with Ceylon, by the chain of rocks obstructing the flow of the ocean. The Vishṇu-Purâṇa says, *badhwâ châmbhonidhim*, " having bridged the ocean," and the Mahâbhârata, iii. 16312, *setubandham akârayat*, " he caused a uniting causeway to be made."

|| Mythological chief of feathered creatures.

the ground, is looking up, immediately the crow and quail are perceived. Thereupon scared by him, the crow fled away; (but) the slow-going quail was caught by him (and) killed. Hence I say: "Not to be travelled with," &c. After that I said: "Brother parrot! why speakest thou so? In my estimation your Honour (is) even as the revered feet of Majesty." Says the parrot: "That may be so; but—

25. Even kind (words) being uttered with smiles by the wicked, excite my fears; like unseasonable flowers.

And (thy) villany (is) made manifest even by thy conversation. For, in the (event of) war between these two, your speech (will be) certainly the primary cause (of it). See:

26. On a fault being committed even openly, a fool, by conciliation, is tranquillized. A wheelwright placed on (his) head his wife and her paramour.

The king asked: "How (was) that?" The parrot related (as follows):—There was, in the city of Prosperity, a wheelwright named Dull-wit; and he knew his wife (to be) unchaste; but had not seen (her) alone with her paramour, with his own eyes. Afterwards, the wheelwright, desirous to see, said: "To-day I shall go (to) another village," (and) started out; (but) having gone a certain distance, he returned secretly, (and) getting under the bed in his own house, remained (there). Now through the confidence engendered (by thinking) thus: "My husband (is) gone (to) another village," the paramour was invited by the wife, in the evening. Afterwards the wheelwright's wife, whilst sporting fearlessly on the bed with that paramour, from a slight touch of the body of her husband crouched under the bed, perceiving her roguish husband, was dejected. The paramour then remarked: "How (is it)? thou art not sporting with me freely to-day? thou appearest as it were dismayed." Then she replied: "Thou (art) an ignorant fellow. He who (is) the lord of my life, (even) he to-day (is) gone to another village. Without him, this village, though ever so full of people, in my opinion appears like a wilderness. What will happen (to him) while dwelling there among strangers? what has he eaten, or where has he lodged? (with) such (thoughts) my heart is rent." Said the paramour: "Then (is) this thy quarrelsome husband such an object of affection as this?" "O blockhead! what art thou saying? Listen:—

27. That woman (is) a virtuous wife who, even spoken to severely or looked at with angry eyes, (maintains) a very placid countenance.

Besides:—
28. Beatific realms (are the portion) of those women whose husband (is) beloved, whether (he be) citizen or forester, sinner or saint.

Again:—
29. A husband (is) indeed the best ornament of a woman, without (other) ornaments. She, though ornamented, deprived of him, shines not.

Thou, an evil-minded paramour, from caprice of mind, art occasionally used, like a flower, betel, (or) sandal-wood; but he, my husband, the taker of my hand, although far away (is) able to sell me to the gods or to give (me) to the Brahmans. What (need) of much (argument)? There is a promise (to this effect),—In him living I live, and on his dying I will follow after. For :—

30. Three krorîs and half a krorî (are) the hairs which (are) on a man,—so many years she dwells in Paradise who follows after her husband (in death).

Again :—

31. As a snake-charmer draws up a snake from (his) hole by force, in the same manner, taking her husband from (Pâtâla), she enjoys (felicity) with him.

Besides :—

32. The loving one who, having embraced (her) lifeless husband, resigns her body on the funeral pile, having effaced even a hundred thousand sins, taking (her) husband, she shall enjoy the realm of the gods.

For :—

33. To whom the father should give (her), or the brother with the father's consent, him she should obey (while) living, and should not dishonour (when) dead.

Hearing all this, the wheelwright having settled (the matter) thus in (his) mind,— "I (am) lucky who (have) such a wife as this, sweetly-spoken (and) affectionate to (her) husband,"—placing the bedstead with the man and woman in it on (his) head, Dull-wit danced about delighted. Hence I say, "On a fault being committed openly," &c.

Then that king having honoured (me) in the usual manner, I was dismissed. The parrot also is now coming after me. Knowing all this, let what is proper to be done be investigated." The prime-minister the ruddy-goose scoffingly said : "Sire! (by) just going to a foreign country, the king's work has been (indeed) executed by the crane, to the extent of his ability. But such (is) the nature of fools. For :—

34. "One should yield a hundred (points), not quarrel,"—such (is) the opinion of the wise. "A contention without even a cause,"—this is the sign of a fool.

The king said : "Enough (of) this censuring of by-gones; let the matter in hand be attended to." The ruddy-goose replied: "Sire! I (will) speak in private. For :—

35. By colour, form, and sound, even by change in the eye (or) mouth, the wise infer the thoughts (of others) : therefore, one should consult in secret.

The king and the minister then remained there; the others went elsewhere. Says the ruddy-goose: "Sire! I am of opinion that by the instigation of some officer of our own this has been done by the crane. For :—

36. A sick man (is) the best (subject) for physicians; a profligate one, for the officers; a fool (is) a living for the wise; a contentious person, for a king."

The king said: "Be it so; the cause in this case should be investigated afterwards; at the present moment speak about what (is) to be done." The ruddy-goose replied: "Let a spy just go there; then we (shall) know his aim, strength, and weakness. For indeed :—

37. A spy should be (engaged) in discovering what (is) to be done and not to be done in his own and foreign countries. He (is) the king's eye. He who has not one, is indeed blind.

And let him go, taking (with him) a second, a confidential (assistant); so that, he himself remaining there, having very secretly ascertained the counsels and actions relating to that place, (and) imparted (them), let him send forth (that) second (one). Thus it is said :—

38. (A king) should communicate with his emissaries, having the appearance of ascetics, under the pretext of studying holy books, at places of pilgrimage, hermitages, and temples.

And a secret emissary (is) one who travels by water or by land; therefore, let this same crane be appointed, (and) let just such another crane as he (is) be (also) sent as a companion, and let the people of his household wait at the king's gate (as hostages);" but, Sire! this sort of thing must be done very secretly. For :—

39. Six-eared council is divulged and (is) picked up by common report: (therefore) with himself and another (only) a king should take counsel.

Besides:—
40. The mischiefs which befall a king through breach of counsel, cannot be repaired: Such (is) the opinion of those skilled in polity."

The king, having reflected, said : " I have found just such a spy." The minister replied : " Sire ! victory in the war (is) already gained." Hereupon a warder having entered (and) saluted said : " Sire ! let attention be paid. A parrot come from Jambu-dwipa waits at the door." The king looks the ruddy-goose in the face. The ruddy-goose said: " Let him go (and) remain awhile in an apartment ; by and by (he is) to be brought in (and) seen." "As your highness commands," having said which, taking the parrot, the warder departed. "So," said the king, " war (is) imminent." " Still, Sire ! " replied the ruddy-goose, " hasty war (is) not the rule.

41. (Is) he a prudent minister who, at the very outset, without consideration, recommends the king either preparation for war or abandoning the country ?

Besides:—
42. One should strive to conquer enemies, (but) never by war; because the victory between two (parties) combating is seen (to be) uncertain.

Again :—
43. By conciliation, by bribes, by dissension,—by these (means), either combined or separately, one should strive to overcome enemies ; (but) never by war.

For :—
44. Every person, forsooth, (is) a hero who has not engaged in war. Who, not perceiving the strength of the enemy, may not be conceited ?

Moreover :—
45. A block of stone is not so (well) lifted by a living being, as by a lever. From a small expedient, a great result; this (is) the great advantage of counsel.

But perceiving war imminent, let there be action. For :—

46. As from seasonable preparation husbandry becomes faithful, so this (art of) polity fructifies after a time, not immediately.

Besides :—

47. Anxiety when at a distance, courage when close at hand, (is) the quality of the great ; in misfortune, the great evince fortitude in the world.

Again :—

48. The first obstacle of all successes (is) certainly undue warmth. Although exceedingly cold, does not water penetrate the surface of the earth ?

And especially, Sire ! (because) this king Spotted-colour, sovereign of the peacocks, (is) very powerful. For :—

49. There is not (such) a precept (as) this: "One should fight with the strong." A combat between an elephant and men (is) not like a foot-fight.

Again :—

50. He (is) a fool, who, not having found a (suitable) opportunity, engages in antagonism. A quarrel with the strong (is) like soaring with insect's wings.

Moreover :—

51. A politic (soldier) having withdrawn (to) a tortoise-like shelter, should endure the (first) shock; but (having) found an opportunity, he should rise up like a cruel serpent.

Listen, Sire !

52. One skilled in expedients can be equally successful over the great as well as over the little ; as the current of a stream (is able) to uproot (both) trees (and) grasses.

Hence having soothed this parrot-envoy let him be detained here until the fort is prepared. For :—

53. One bowman stationed (behind) a rampart is made to combat a hundred ; a hundred (can combat) ten thousand ; therefore, a fortress is recommended.

Moreover :—

54. Of what enemy (is) not an unfortified country an object of contempt ? A king without a fort (is) helpless, like a man fallen out of a ship.

55. He should construct a fort, with a great moat, surrounded by a high rampart, having engines, water, and rock, with the protection of a river, a desert, and a forest.

56. Spaciousness, extreme inaccessibility, a store of liquid, grain, and fuel, (with) both ingress and egress; (these are) the seven excellencies of a fort.

The king said : " In the preparation of the fort, who should be appointed ? "

The ruddy-goose replied :—

57. " Whoever (is) skilful in work him should one there appoint. Whoever has not had experience, although conversant with the sciences, is bewildered in practical matters.

Therefore, let General Heron be called. Upon this being done, the king, looking at the Heron (when) present, said : " O Heron ! hastily make ready the fort." The

Heron having saluted said: "Sire! as to the fort, that truly for a long time has been prepared. (It is) a great lake. But let a store of eatable things be collected in the island in its midst. For:—

58. A store of grain, O king! (is) better than every (other) store. A jewel thrown into the mouth would not effectuate the sustaining of life.

Moreover:—
59. Of all flavours salt is renowned (as) the best flavour; without that, O king! sauce is as cow-dung."

The king said: "O General Heron! go quickly, let everything be prepared." Then the warder having again entered said: "Sire! there waits at the door the king of the crows, named Cloud-colour, come from Ceylon. Attended by a retinue he does homage, (and) wishes to see the king's feet." The king said: "The crow (is) wise, and has seen much; therefore he is to be received, this is understood." The ruddy-goose replied: "Sire! that may be so; but the crow (is) a land-goer, of a different party to us; therefore, he is engaged on the side of our opponents. How (then) is he to be received? Thus it is said:—

60. The fool who, after abandoning his own party, delights in the opposite party, is slain by those strangers, like the blue-coloured jackal."

The king asked: "How (was) that?" The minister relates (as follows):—There was a certain jackal rambling at his pleasure in the outskirts of a town (who) fell into a vat for receiving indigo. Afterwards unable to get out, in the morning, making himself appear like dead, (he) remained (still). Now the owner of the indigo vat, having picked him out, (and) carried (him) to a distance, dropped him. Then he, going to the wood (and) perceiving himself (to be of) a blue colour, (thus) reflected: "I now (am) of the finest hue; therefore, can I not accomplish my elevation?" Having considered thus, the jackals were called together by him, (and) addressed: "Oh! ye denizens of the forest! I have been consecrated to the sovereignty of the woods, with an extract of every medicinal herb, by the very hand of the adorable goddess of the forest. Behold my colour. Therefore, beginning from this day, proceedings should be conducted in this forest by my command." Now the jackals, perceiving him of an excellent colour, reverentially prostrated themselves (and) said: "As your Majesty commands." Thus by this process his sovereignty among all the dwellers in the forest was (established). Subsequently, surrounded by his own kindred, supremacy was accomplished by him. Afterwards, having obtained a superior retinue (of) lions, tigers, &c., looking at the jackals in the assembly (and) despising (them), he removed his own kinsmen to a distance, being ashamed (of them). Thereupon, perceiving the jackals dejected, an old jackal promised (thus): "Do not despond, if we who know the vulnerable points are despised by this (fellow) ignorant of policy. It can be arranged by me so that he is destroyed. Since these tigers and the rest, deceived solely by the colour, not knowing (him to be) a jackal, imagine him (to be) a king; therefore do something whereby he is (to be) detected. (This) should be carried out in the way I say. All of you, at eventide, in his vicinity all at once set up a great yell; then having heard that noise, naturally by him also a cry (will) be made. For :—

61. Whatever the natural disposition of anyone may be, that (is) hard to be overcome (by) him. If a dog were made a king, would he not gnaw a shoe?

Then having recognised (him) by the voice, (he will) be killed by the tiger. On this being done, that (event) happened. Thus (it) is said :—

62. An enemy of one's own species knows every defect, vulnerable point, and bravery; and, being inside, he consumes, like fire (consumes) a dry tree.

Hence I say, "From abandoning one's own party," &c. The king said: "Although (it be) so, still let him just be seen; he (is) come from afar; in his reception (afterwards) deliberation should be made." The ruddy-goose observed: "Sire! a spy has been appointed, and the fort put in order; hence, having seen the parrot (and) having given (him) an answer, let him be sent forth. But :—

63. Chânakya slew Nanda,* by employing an active envoy; therefore (a king) surrounded by (his) warriors should see an ambassador, separated by a wide space."

Then, an audience being arranged, the parrot was called, (and) the crow also. The parrot with head a little raised, having seated (himself on) the seat provided, says: "Sir Gold-egg! the great king of kings Spotted-colour, lord of the peacocks, (whose) lotus-feet are illuminated by dazzling strings of rubies in the crowns of all (prostrate) monarchs, commands thee, (thus): 'If thou hast (any) occasion for life or fortune, then having come hastily, salute my feet; otherwise bethink thee (of) starting off (to) another place.'" Having heard that, the king angrily said: "Ha! is there no one in the assembly before us who strangles him?" Then Cloud-colour starting up said: "Sire! command (me), and I (will) slay this vile parrot." (But) the minister said: "Not so, worthy Sir! Listen awhile—

64. That (is) not a council where there are no elders; they (are) not elders who do not know law; that (is) not law where there is no truth; whatever fear influences (is) not truth.

For this truly (is) law:

65. An ambassador, although a barbarian, should be inviolable; for the king (speaks by) the mouth of the ambassador. Even among uplifted weapons an ambassador speaks not otherwise (than his message).

Besides :—

66. Who infers his own inferiority (or) another's superiority by the assertions of an ambassador? By his inviolable character an ambassador always states the whole (of his message)."

Then the king and the crow recovered (their) natural temper; and the parrot hastily arising withdrew. Afterwards, having conducted (him back), apologized, and having presented (him) with gold, ornaments, and the like, the parrot was dismissed by the ruddy-goose. He returned (to) his own country. Then having reached the Vindhya mountains, he saluted his own king Spotted-colour. King Spotted-colour having perceived him said: "Parrot! what news? What (is) that country like?" The parrot replied: "Sire! shortly, this news,—preparation for war is now to be

---

* Chânakya was a Brâhman who conspired and succeeded in dethroning the Nanda dynasty. He placed a robber Chandragupta on the throne in the time of Alexander the Great.

made; and that country, the island of Camphor, (is) a district of Paradise. How can it be described?" The king, having convened all the chiefs, sat down to deliberate. Thus it is said:—

67. A discontented Brahman (and) a contented king (are) always ruined: a modest harlot and an immodest woman of family (are) ruined.

The minister, a vulture named Far-seeing, (then) said: "A war unrighteously (waged is) not just. For:—

68. When friends, ministers, and allies, should be firm in their attachment, and (those) of the enemies the reverse, then should war be made.

Besides:—
69. Territory, a friend, and gold, (constitute) the triple fruit of war; when these are certain to result, then should war be made."

The king said: "Let the minister meanwhile inspect my forces; thus let their readiness be ascertained. Then let the astrologer be called, (and) let him determine the auspicious moment for marching." Says the minister: "Sire! still hastily marching (is) improper. For:—

70. Fools who begin hastily without having considered the enemy's strength, they most certainly receive the embrace of the edge of a sword.

"Minister," said the king, "do not repress my energy on every occasion. Point out the way in which one desirous of conquest subjugates another's country." The vulture said: "Sire! I (will) declare that; but only (when) followed (is) it fruitful. Thus it is said ı—

71. What (use is) advice like the S'âstras (to) a king (when) not followed? Nowhere can there be the cure of a disease from the (mere) knowledge of medicines.

And the king's command (is) not to be disobeyed, therefore I declare what I have heard. Listen, Sire!

72. Among rivers, mountains, forests, and forts, wherever (there is) danger, O king! there the commander should go, with forces drawn up in array.

73. The superintendent of the force should go in front, accompanied by the bravest men; in the centre (are) the women, the king, the treasure, and whatever force (is) weak.

74. On both flanks, the horse; the chariots on the flanks of the horse; on the flanks of the chariots, the elephants; and (on the flanks) of the elephants, the foot-soldiers.

75. Behind should march the commander, encouraging now and then the dispirited, associated with counsellors and warriors, the king taking an army—

76. Should traverse swampy (and) mountainous country with elephants; the level (ground), with horses; the water, with boats; everywhere, with foot-soldiers.

77. The marching of elephants (is) pronounced best on the approach of the rains; (that) of horses at any other (time) than that; (that) of foot-soldiers at all times.

78. Among mountains (and) difficult passes, the protection of the king should be attended to: although protected by his warriors, (his) sleep (should be on a par) with the sleep of a Yogin.*

79. He should destroy, he should drag the enemy through difficult passes, thorny brakes, and mire: on entering the enemy's territory, he should place the pioneers in front.

80. Where the king (is), there (should be) the treasury; without treasure (there is) no royalty. He should give (liberally) to warriors. Who does not fight for the generous?

For:—

81. Man (is) not the slave of man, O king! but of wealth. Importance and insignificance (are) connected with wealth and poverty.

82. Without breaking (ranks) they should fight and should protect each other. Whatsoever part of the army is weak he should place in the centre of the array.

83. And the king should cause the foot-soldiers to fight in the van of the army; and having blockaded the foe he should sit, and should desolate his country.

84. On the level he should combat with chariots and horse; on watery places, also with boats and elephants; on (firm) ground, in places covered by trees and bushes, with bows, swords, shields, and (other) weapons.

85. He should always spoil his (enemy's) grain, food, water, and fuel; he should also break down his tanks, ramparts, and trenches.

86. Among forces, the chief (is) the elephant; for a king (there is) none other like him. With his own limbs merely, an elephant (is) recognised (as possessing) eight weapons.

87. The horse (is) the strength of armies; (and is) considered a moving rampart; therefore, a king superior in cavalry (is) victorious in a land-fight.

Thus it has been said:—

88. Those fighting mounted on horseback are hard to conquer even (by) the gods; their enemies though dwelling afar are in their hands.

89. The primary means of carrying on war (is) the preservation of the entire army; the clearing of the roads of the country they call the business of the infantry.

90. Naturally heroic, skilled in arms, not disloyal, superior to fatigue, (consisting)

---

* That is, brief and light.

chiefly of renowned Kshatriyas,—(this) they consider the most excellent force.

91. By the bestowal of even much riches, men on earth do not (fight) so (well), as they fight (for) the honour conferred by the chief, O king!

92. Better a small choice army, not a multitude of heads: the overthrow of the weaklings would evidently cause the overthrow of the best (troops).

93. Unkindness, absence, appropriation of the share which should have been distributed, procrastination, non-requital,—these are the causes of estrangement.

94. One desirous of conquest should march against the enemy, without distressing (his) army; an army fatigued by long marches is easily overthrown (by) the enemy.

95. There is no better advice (for) causing division among enemies than (the setting up of) a claimant (to the throne); therefore, one should assiduously raise up the enemy's heir.

96. Having formed an alliance with either the heir-apparent or the prime-minister he should excite the inward wrath of the firm-minded enemy.

97. And he should cause the false ally to be slain, either by overthrowing (him) in battle, or by capturing and carrying off his cattle, after imprisoning his chief dependants.

98. A king should populate his own territory, though despoiling his enemy's country; or else, (that enemy's country) colonized with liberality and respect, certainly (becomes) lucrative."

The king said: "Ah! what (will accrue) with much (being) said ɪ

99. One's own rise (and) the enemy's fall; the two (constitute) polity :—thus much (sums it up). (While) admitting this, (the worth of) the eloquent harangue is proved by actions."

The minister laughingly said: "All this (is) true; but—

100. One nature (is) ungovernable; another (is) restrained by moral laws. Whence (can arise) a common predicament for both light and darkness?"

At length rising up, the king set forth at the time declared auspicious by the astrologers. Now a messenger despatched by the spy, coming to Gold-egg (and) saluting, said: "Sire! king Spotted-colour (is) almost arrived; now he is actually encamped at the foot of the Malaya mountains; let the preparation of the fortress be immediately attended to, for that vulture (is) a great minister. Besides, (in) the course of his confidential conversation with someone, I have got at this hint, that (there is) already somebody employed by him in our fort." The ruddy-goose said: "Sire! this must be the crow." The king replied: "That (can) never (be); if so, then why did he make preparation for the overthrow of the parrot? Besides, his efforts for war (have been) since the coming of the parrot, and he has been here a long time." Says the minister: "Nevertheless, a new-comer (is) to be doubted." The king said: "Even new-comers appear to be requiters of favours. Listen:—

101. Even a kind stranger (is) a kinsman; an unkind kinsman (is) a stranger. Unkind (is) the sickness generated in (one's own) body; (but) kindly (is) the medicine found in the woods.

Again:—

102. Of king Low-caste there was a servant named Best-of-heroes; he, in a very little time offered up his own son."

The minister asked: "How (is) that?" The king related (as follows):—Formerly, in a pleasure-lake belonging to king Low-caste, I was much attached (to) Sprig-of-Camphor, the daughter of the flamingo named Camphor-sport. There, a Râjpût named Best-of-Heroes, having arrived from some country, approached the warder at the palace-gate (and) said: "I (am) a Râjpût seeking a livelihood; procure me a sight of the king." Then introduced by him (into) the royal presence, he said: "Sire! if there is need (of) me (as) a servant, then let my pay be provided." Low-caste said: "What (is) thy pay?" Best-of-heroes replied: "Four hundred suvarnas a-day." The king asked: "What (is) thy equipment?" Best-of-heroes replied: "Two arms; and for a third, a sword." The king, reflecting an instant, said surprisedly: "Friend, that (is) not possible." Hearing that Best-of-heroes saluted (and) departed. Now (this) was said by (his) advisers: "Sire! giving the hire of four days, let his character be ascertained, whether he (is) useful (that) he takes so much hire, or (is) useless." Then, from the advice of the ministers, having recalled (him, and) presented (him with) betel* he gave those wages. For:—

103. Betel (is) pungent, bitter, spicy, sweet, alkaline, astringent, a carminative, antiphlegmatic, a vermifuge, a remover of the defect of foul breath; the ornament of the mouth, a detergent, the kindler of the flame of love;—these thirteen virtues of betel, O friend! (are) hard to obtain even in heaven.

And the application of the stipend was secretly watched by the king. One half of it was shared by Best-of-heroes among the gods and the Brâhmans; half of the remainder, among the afflicted; the rest (was consumed) with expenses of food and amusement. Having done all this (as) a constant practice, day and night he attends, sword in hand, (at) the king's gate; and when the king himself commands, then he goes to his own house. Now one night, on the fourteenth of the dark (half of the month), the king heard a piteous lamenting sound. Hearing that, the king cries: "Who (is there)? who attends here at the gate?" Then he answered: "Sire! (it is) I, Best-of-heroes." Then the king said: "Let the lamenting be pursued." Best-of-heroes, having exclaimed, "As the king commands," set forth. Then the king thought: "This solitary Râjpût has been sent by me into darkness which may be pierced with a needle: that (is) improper. I, also, going (will) see what it (is)." Thereupon the

---

* Presented on the completion of an agreement.

king also taking a sword, in the course of following (him) passed out of the gate of the city. Then, going along, a certain weeping female, endowed with youth and beauty, and adorned with every ornament, was seen by Best-of-heroes, and questioned: "Who (art) thou? for what art thou grieving?" The woman replied: "I (am) the Fortune of this king Low-caste. For a long time, under the shadow of his arm, with much happiness (I have) reposed. On the third day the king will reach dissolution. I shall become protectorless, I shall remain no longer; therefore, I weep." Best-of-heroes said: "By what means is your Grace's dwelling here still (to be effected)?" The Fortune (of the king) replied: "If thou, with thy own hand, having cut off the head of thine own son Energetic, possessed of the thirty-two marks of a hero, make an offering (to) the revered All-auspicious one,* then the king will remain a hundred years, (and) I (shall) dwell happily." Having said this she became invisible. Then the delighted Best-of-heroes went to his own house, and awakened his soundly sleeping wife and son. They both, shaking off sleep, sat up, (and) Best-of-heroes related the whole of the speech of (the king's) Fortune. Hearing that Energetic said with delight: Fortunate (am) I of whom (there is) such a fitness for the preservation of (my) prince's kingdom! Father! what now (is) the cause of delay? Since, at any time, in such a service as this, the abandoning of this body (is) praiseworthy.

104. A wise man would give up riches and even life for the sake of another. Death being inevitable, better the abandonment (of life) for the sake of the good.

The mother of Energetic said: "O husband! if this is not to be done for the benefit of our king, then by what other act will there be a requital of the high salary (you receive)." Having thus reflected, they all went to the temple of the All-auspicious one. There, having worshipped the All-auspicious one, Best-of-heroes said: "Goddess! be favourable. Let the great king Low-caste be victorious! Let this offering be accepted!" Having said which, he struck off his son's head. Then Best-of-heroes reflected: "An exact acquittance has been made for the salary received from the king; now life without (my) son (is) a burden." Thinking thus, he cut off his own head. Then his wife, also, through grief for her husband and son, did the same. Hearing and seeing all this, the king with astonishment reflected:—

105. "Insignificant creatures like me are born and die; (but) the like unto this (man) has not been in the world, nor will be.

Therefore, deprived of him, what advantage (accrues) even with a kingdom (at disposal)," saying this Low-caste flourished a sword to cut off his own head. Then the compassionate, revered, all-auspicious one, manifesting herself, seized on the king's hand:—"Son! enough (of) this rashness; there is now (to be) no injury to thy kingdom." The king, prostrating (himself) reverently said: "O Goddess! there is no (further) use for me with kingdom, or life, or prosperity. If I (am) deserving of compassion, then by the (sacrifice of the) remainder of my life, let this distinguished minister my servant the Rájpút, with his wife and son, live (again); otherwise I will attain the condition (they) have reached." The Revered one said: "With this thy

---

* The goddess Durgá.

true excellence and affection for a servant I am everyway gratified. Go; be victorious! Let this Râjpût, with his family, also live!" Thereupon Best-of-heroes, with (his) son and wife, restored to life, went home. The king, unseen by them, regained the terrace of the palace (and) laid down as before. Then Best-of-heroes standing at the gate, again questioned by the king, replied: "Sire! the weeping woman having perceived me became invisible. There is no other news whatever." Hearing his speech the king with astonishment reflected: "How can this exalted creature be commended (sufficiently)? For:—

106. The noble should speak kindly; the hero should be a non-boaster; the liberal should rain upon the excellent; the brave should be gentle.

This (is) the characteristic of a great man. In him is all (this found). Then the king in the morning, having convened a special court, declared all the events of the (preceding) night, approvingly conferred upon him the kingdom of the Carnatic.

Why, then, (is) a new-comer necessarily an enemy? Among them also there are good, bad, and indifferent." The ruddy-goose said:—

107. "(Is) he a minister who, to please the king, counsels what ought not to be done as though it ought to be done: better wound the feelings of the king, but not (bring about) his destruction by what should not be done.

108. The king of whom the physician, spiritual guide, and minister (are) flatterers, is quickly deprived of body, virtue, and treasure.

Listen, O king!

109. 'What has been obtained by one (person) through virtue, that also will be for me.' From infatuation (arising) herefrom, a wealth-seeking barber, having struck down a beggar, was killed."

The king asked: "How (was) that?" The minister related (as follows):—There was, in the city of Oudh, a soldier named Crest-jewel. He, desirous of wealth, with pain of body, for a long time propitiated the Revered one whose crest-jewel is the half-moon.* Afterwards, purified from his sins, having a revelation in sleep, through the favour of S'ambhu,† he was commanded by the Lord of Yakshas‡ (thus):—"O prince of soldiers! to-day, having caused (thyself) to be shaved, thou wilt station thyself (staff in hand) secretly at the door of thy house. Then whatever beggar thou seest come into the fore-court, him thou wilt mercilessly slay with blows of (thy) staff; thereupon that beggar will instantly become a jar full of gold, with which thou and thy family, as long as you live, can remain happily." Thereafter, on that being done, that (which was declared) came to pass. Then the barber who had been brought to shave him, having seen all (that occurred) reflected: "Ho! this (is) the contrivance for getting a treasure! then why am I not doing so also?" From thenceforward, the barber, every day, in that fashion, (with) a club in his hand, looked out for the arrival of a beggar. Once having met with a beggar in that way, striking him with the club, he killed (him). Through that crime the barber himself was beaten by the king's officers, and died. Hence I say: "What by one has been obtained through virtue," &c. The king said:—

---

* S'iva.   † The god S'iva.   ‡ Kuvera, the god of wealth.

110. By bringing up tales of former occurrences is it determined whether a stranger is a friend without a motive, or a betrayer of confidence?

Go to! go to! let preparation be (now) made. A king named Spotted-colour is now encamped on the table-land of the Malaya (mountains); therefore what is now to be done?" The minister said: "Sire! it was heard by me, from the mouth of the spy (just) arrived, that Spotted-colour has placed no esteem on the advice of the prime-minister the vulture; hence the fool (is) easily to be conquered.

Thus it has been said :—
111. The covetous, the cruel, the intractable, the untruthful, the careless, the timid, the wavering, the foolish, the despiser of (antogonistic) warriors,—is known (as) an enemy easy to be cut up.

Therefore as long as he is not blockading my fort, let the Heron and other generals be appointed to destroy his forces in the rivers, mountains, forests, and roads. Thus it has been said :—

112. Fatigued by long marches, perplexed by rivers, mountains, and forests, terrified by the fear of dreadful fires, enfeebled by hunger and thirst,—

113. the furious, straitened for provisions, wasted with sickness and famine, scattered, not very numerous, distressed by rain and wind,—

114. bespattered with mud, dust, and water, greatly perplexed, scattered by brigands,—an enemy's army thus circumstanced, the king should destroy.

Besides :—
115. The king should always smite an army overpowered by fatigue, sleeping in the day-time, worn out by watching from fear of a (night) assault.

Hence, going (against) the army of that negligent one, as opportunity (serves), let the Heron and the rest smite (it) day and night." On this being done, many of Spotted-colour's troops and officers were slain. Then Spotted-colour, dejected, said to Far-seeing his minister : "Father! has neglect of me been committed by thee? or is there anywhere indiscretion (on) our (part)? Thus it has been said :—

116. "The kingdom (is) gained,"—(thinking) so, one should not act indiscreetly. Indiscretion destroys prosperity, as decay (destroys) the finest beauty.

Besides :—
117. The clever one gains fortune; the wholesome-eater, health; the healthy, happiness; the persevering, the limit of knowledge; the discreet, virtue, wealth, and fame."

The vulture said : " Sire, pay attention :—
118. Even an ignorant king, by attending to one of accomplished learning, obtains excellent prosperity; as a tree close to water.

Again :—

119. Drinking, women, hunting, gaming, the unjust seizure of property, violence both of censure and of punishment,—(these are) the vices of kings.

Moreover :—

120. Great successes are not to be obtained by one following the sole impulse of courage, nor by one whose inward soul is at a loss for expedients : Prosperity resides in both policy and bravery (combined).

Perceiving the energy of thy own troops, inclined only to inconsiderate haste, thou hast despised counsels though suggested by me, and (hast used) harsh language : hence this fruit of bad policy is experienced by your Highness. Thus it has been said :—

121. What bad minister do not errors of policy overtake ? What eater of unwholesome things do not sicknesses afflict ? Whom does prosperity not inflate with pride ? Whom does not death kill ? Whom do sensual pleasures excited by women not torment ?

122. Sadness destroys mirth ; the winter, autumn ; the sun, darkness ; ingratitude, good deeds ; the manifestation of kindness, grief ; (good) policy, misfortune ; bad policy, prosperous fortune."

Therefore I reflected (thus) : "Ah ! woe the day ! this peacock-king (is) destitute of wisdom ; else why is he darkening with the torch of (his own) talk, the moonlight of narratives of politic science. For :—

123. What (will) he do (with) literature who has no sense of his own ? what will a lamp do for one deprived of both eyes ?

For that (reason) I remained silent." Then the king, (with) clasped hands, becoming aware of his own fault, respectfully said : " Father ! let this fault be mine ; now quickly inform me how, with the remainder of the force, I (may) retreat (and) reach the Vindhya mountains." The vulture thinks (thus) within himself : " Here a remedy (is) to be devised. For :—

124. Anger should always be restrained (if felt) towards the gods, a spiritual guide, cows, kings, Bráhmans, the young, old, or afflicted."

And he says smilingly : " Sire ! be not afraid ; be of good cheer ! Listen, Sire !

125. The skill of counsellors is manifested in the re-union of what has been severed ; of physicians, in a complication (of diseases). Who (is) not clever when an affair (is) prosperous ?

Besides :—

126. Even in a small undertaking, the little-minded easily become bewildered ; but those of mature mind, great in undertakings, stand unmoved.

Sire ! through thy valour, having destroyed the fort, I (will) in no long time lead thee to the Vindhya mountains, with fame, dignity, and strength." The king said : " How is that now to be accomplished with (so) very small a force ? " The vulture replied: "Sire! it will all be (done). Since promptitude for one desirous of conquest (is) the essential requisite for the accomplishment of victory, therefore, to-day let the gate of the fort be blockaded. Now Gold-egg's spy the crane, having returned, reported: "Sire! truly with very little force, king Spotted-colour, relying on the advice of the vulture, having come will blockade the gate of the fort." The flamingo said: "Sir Know-all! what now is to be done?" The ruddy-goose replied: "There should be no fear; let the efficient and non-efficient of our own force be tested; having ascertained that, let conciliatory gifts of gold, dresses, &c., be made, according to deserts. For thus (it) has been said :—

127. Fortune does not desert that lion-like prince who should withhold even a misapplied cowrie, (as though) equal to a thousand nishkas, (but who is) open-handed in (respect of) crores, at (proper) times.

Besides :—

128. On eight (occasions) there is not (such a thing as) excessive expenditure; (that is to say), on a sacrifice, on a marriage, on distress, on the reduction of an enemy, on an act producing fame, on the reception of friends, on a beloved wife, (and) on indigent relations.

For :—

129. A fool, from fear of a very little expenditure, brings about the loss of all. What sensible person would abandon the merchandise through excessive fear of the toll?"

The king asked: "How, at the present time, is prodigality appropriate? It has been said, 'One should preserve wealth against misfortune.'" The minister replied: "Whence (can come) misfortune for the fortunate?" The king observed: "Sometimes fortune is fickle." The minister rejoined: "Sire! hoarded wealth vanishes; therefore, Sire! abandoning parsimony let your best warriors be preferred with gifts and honours. Thus it has been said :—

130. (Soldiers) knowing each other; pleased; regardless of life; resolute; of good family; (if properly) honoured, conquer entirely the force of the enemy.

Besides :—

131. Warriors, well-disposed, closely knit, resolute; although (but) five hundred heroes, they crush the hosts of the enemy.

Moreover :—

132. A mean, indiscriminating, fierce, (and) ungrateful man is shunned by the honest, (and) by (his own) wife also; how much more (is he) not (shunned) by others!

For :—

133. Truth, bravery, and also liberality; these (are) the three qualities of kings; abandoned by these a king assuredly incurs censure.

On such an occasion as the present ministers, at least, should be advanced. Thus it has been said :—

134. With whomsoever one may be intimately associated, with him (is) mounting and falling; fully trusted, (he) should be employed in (matters of) life and death.

For :—

135. Of whatever king the ministers are a rogue, a woman, or a child, tossed by the winds of bad policy, he sinks in an ocean of cares.

Observe, O king!

136. (He) whose pleasure and anger (are) restrained, and (whose) treasury (is subject to) very slight expenditure, and (who is) continually regardful of servants,—the earth is for him a giver of wealth.

137. A king should never despise politic ministers, whose rise and decline is firmly (connected) with (those of) the monarch.

For :—

138. The support of a hand from firm ground is given by faithful counsellors, for a king blinded by passion sinking in an ocean of cares."

Now Cloud-colour, having approached and saluted said : " Sire! favour (me) with a glance. This enemy the peacock desirous of war is actually at the gate of the fort; therefore, if there is a command from the feet of your Majesty, I issuing out (will) manifest my bravery. By that means, I (shall) approach acquittance of the debt of your Majesty's favour." The ruddy-goose says : " Not so. If (by) going out (there is) to be fighting, then the refuge of the fort (becomes) useless. See, for example :—

139. Although ferocious as (he is), a crocodile come out from the water (is) powerless ; truly, even a lion strayed from the wood, would be like a jackal."

The minister said : " Sire! going yourself let the fight be inspected. For :—

140. Having advanced the army, the king while looking on should incite it to fight. Superintended by (his) master, doeš not even a dog certainly play the lion."

Hereupon they all, going to the gate of the fort, produced a desperate encounter. Next day, the king named Spotted-colour said to the vulture: " Father! let thy promise now be performed." The vulture replied : " Listen a little :—

141. The defect of a fortress is stated (as follows)—unable (to hold out for a long) time*; very small ; commanded by a fool or a profligate ; unprotected ; and (with) timid soldiers.

That, however, is not here (the case).

142. These (are) declared (to be) the four expedients for the capture of a fort,—sowing dissension, a protracted siege, an assault, (and) daring heroism.

And here effort must be made to the extent of (our) power." Spotted-colour said : " Even so." Then upon the sun being risen early in the morning, whilst the tight was going on at the four gates, fire was thrown simultaneously by the crows into every house within the fort. Then hearing a shout " The fort is taken, is taken!" and seeing fire evidently kindled in several of the houses, many soldiers of the flamingo, and other dwellers in the fort also, hastily entered the water. For :—

143. Good counsel, good courage, good battle, good retreat, at an appropriate time, one should effect to the extent of one's power ; and should not hesitate.

The flamingo, from (his) easy nature (was) slow in motion, and attended by the heron, being approached by the cock, a general of Spotted-colour, was beset. King

---

* If *akál* means "famine," as is the case in Hindî, then this sentence would mean, "suffering famine."

Gold-egg said: "O General Heron! from devotion to me thou shalt not get thyself killed. Now I (am) unable to proceed; thou (art) still able to go; therefore, going, enter the water; and having escaped with the consent of Know-all thou wilt make my son named Crest-jewel king." The heron replied: "Sire! such an unendurable speech should not be uttered. As long as sun and moon exist, so long let the king be victorious. I (am) commandant of your Majesty's fort; therefore, at all events, let the enemy enter by the gate-way stained with my flesh and blood. Besides, O king!

144. A patient, generous, and appreciative master is obtained by good luck."

The king added: "That is so; but—

An honest, clever, and loyal servant (is) indeed very hard to be found."

The heron said: "Listen, Sire!—

145. If, except (in) battle, there were no fear of death, then (it might be) proper to flee elsewhere; but death (is) the inevitable (lot) of living creatures, why should one tarnish fame uselessly?

Besides:—

146. In this world, perishable as the whirling of waves agitated by the wind, the spending of life for the benefit of another arises by reason of virtue (in a former birth).

Then, Sire! the prince is always to be preserved.

147. Even the most prosperous *prakriti*,* abandoned by (her) lord, lives not. What can even the physician Dhanwantari† do when life is extinct?

Besides:—

148. On the king closing his eyes, this mortal world collapses, and on his rising, it revives; as on the (rising of) sun, the lotus.

Moreover:—

149. A sovereign, a minister, a territory, a fort, a treasury, an army, an ally, and corporations of citizens, (are) the essentials (constituting) the members of a kingdom.‡

Here, also, the king (is) the chief member.

Now the cock, having approached, inflicted a wound with his very sharp spurs on the body of the flamingo. Then hastily coming up, the heron shielded the king with his own body. Immediately the heron lacerated with blows from the beak and spurs of the cock, having covered the king with his own body, pushed (him) into the water. The cock, also, torn by many thrusts from the beak and blows from the wings, was killed by General Heron. Afterwards the heron also, overpowered by many birds, was slain.

Now Spotted-colour having entered the fort, and having caused the property remaining in the fort to be seized, marched forth, praised by encomiasts with shouts of "Victory."

The princes said: "In that army of the flamingo, the heron (was) truly meritorious; by whom, with the sacrifice of his own life, the king was preserved. For:—

150. Cows generate offspring all shaped like cattle; (but only) an occasional lord of kine, (whose) shoulder is touched by the horn (of the others).

---

* The *s'akti* or female correlative of deity. † The Hindû Esculapius.
‡ These are called the eight *prakritis*, or essentials, of royalty.

Vishṇuśarman said: "May the virtuous enjoy the virtue-purchased imperishable worlds, attended by Vidyâdharîs.* Thus it is said:—

151. Those brave men who, loyal and grateful, for their master's sake sacrifice (their) lives in battles, go to heaven.

152. Wherever a hero (is) slain, encompassed by foes, he obtains imperishable worlds, provided he does not descend to unmanliness.

'War' has (now) been heard, by your Highnesses." The princes exclaimed: "(And) having heard, we are delighted." Vishṇuśarman (then) said: "Moreover, may it be thus also—

153. May there never be war with elephants, horses, and infantry, for your Highnesses! May enemies, scattered by the winds of politic counsels, seek refuge (in) mountain fastnesses!"

Here ends the third chapter of Friendly Advice, called War.

---

* Demi-goddesses who carry the souls of slain warriors to Paradise.

PEACE.

At the time of recommencing the discourse the princes said: "Sir! we have heard 'War;' let Peace now be related." Vishṇuśarman replied: "Attend! I am (about to) relate Peace, of which this is the first verse,—

1. On the great war being stayed between the kings (and) their exhausted armies, by a conference of the two arbitrators, the vulture and the ruddy-goose, peace was immediately made.

The princes asked, how that (occurred), and Vishṇuśarman related (the following particulars):—After (what was said in the last chapter) the flamingo asked: "Who threw fire into my fort? (Was it) by an enemy, or by somebody engaged on the side of the enemy residing in my fort?" The ruddy-goose replied: "Sire! Your Highness's disinterested friend Cloud-colour, with its retinue, is not to be seen here; therefore, I think, this (is) his act." The king reflecting a moment said: "It is even so; this is my bad fortune. And (it) has been thus declared:—

2. This (is) the fault of destiny; assuredly it (is) not (the fault) of counsellors. An affair well (and) carefully planned is spoilt through destiny."

The minister remarked: "This, too, has been said:—

3. A man blames destiny (when) getting into an unhappy state. An ignorant (man) never thinks (it) the fault of his own acts.

Further:—

4. He who heeds not the advice of well-wishing friends perishes, like the foolish turtle (who) dropped from the stick.

The king asked, how that (happened, and) the minister replied:—In the country of Magadha there is a lake called Blooming-lotus; there for a long time dwelt two geese named Slender and Hideous. A friend of theirs, a turtle named Shell-neck, lived hard by. Now once (upon a time, some) fishermen coming there said: "To-day remaining here, early to-morrow we must kill fish, tortoises, and such like." Hearing that the turtle said to the geese: "Friends (you) have heard this conversation of the fishermen, now, then, what is to be done by me?" The geese replied: "First of all, let (the matter be fully) ascertained; afterwards, having well reflected that which is fitting should be done." The turtle replied: "Not so; for I have already witnessed a disaster in this place. And thus it has been said:—

5. Fate-not-come and likewise Ready-wit these two happily escaped; What-will-be perished."

They both asked: "How (was) that?" The turtle replied:—Formerly, in this very lake, upon just such fishermen being prepared, three fishes (thus) consulted (together). One fish named Fate-not-come, said: "This very day I (shall) go (to) another body of water;" saying which he somehow or other with difficulty reached another pool. Another fish named Ready-wit said: "From the absence of evidence, where should I go on account of the future; therefore, when the affair has happened (one) should act according to circumstances. And it has been thus said:—

6. He who can repair a misfortune which has happened is wise; as the paramour (who) was disowned by the merchant's wife before his face.

What-will-be asked, how that (was). Ready-wit related (as follows):—There was, in the city of Valour, a merchant named Sea-given. His wife Jewel-bright by name, was continually sporting with one of the servants. For:—

7. No one is either agreeable or disagreeable for women; as cows in a forest are ever seeking fresh and fresh grass.

Now once this Jewel-bright was seen by Sea-given to be kissing the cheek of the servant. Then the wife instantly approaching her husband said: "Husband! the assurance of this servant (is) great, for he eats the camphor brought for you. I have smelt the perfume of the camphor plainly in his mouth." Thus it is said:—

8. (It is) known (that) the food of women is two-fold, their wit, four-fold; their cunning, six-fold; and their lust, eight-fold.

On hearing this, the servant also pretending offence, said: "How can a servant remain in whosesoever house (there is) such a wife as this, where the mistress is every moment smelling the servant's mouth?" Then, rising up, he went away; thereupon the good man, apologising strenuously with many affectionate speeches, giving presents of betel and such like, having contented (him), brought (him) back. Hence I say, "On a misfortune that has happened," &c. Then What-will-be said:—

9. "What (is) not to be, will not be; if (it is) to be, then (it will) not (be) otherwise (than as ordained). Why is not this medicine, the antidote of anxiety, drunk?"

Then in the morning, Ready-wit caught by the net, making himself appear as if dead, remained (motionless). Thereupon, (he) was thrown out from the net; (but) springing up from the ground, (he) entered deep water. What-will-be, caught by the fishermen, was killed. Hence I say, "Fate-not-come," &c. Therefore let it be arranged to-day how I (may) get to another pool. The geese said: "Upon reaching another body of water (there is) safety for thee; (but) what way (is there) for thy going (there) on land?" The turtle replied: "Let a method be devised by which I (may) go with you by way of the sky." The geese inquired: "How is (that) scheme practicable?" The turtle replied: "I can hang with (my) mouth (to) a stick held in the beaks by you two; in this way, by the strength of your wings I also can go easily. The geese rejoined: "This scheme is practicable. Let it be so. Still:—

10. A wise man while thinking (over) a scheme, should think also (about) disaster. The young ones of a fool of a crane (who was) looking on, were eaten by ichneumons."

The turtle asked: "How (was) that?" The geese related (as follows):— Towards the north there is a mountain called Vulture-cliff; (and) cranes are living there in a fig-tree on the banks of the Revâ; a snake, also, dwells in a hole at the foot of that fig-tree, and he (habitually) devours the young of the cranes. Then hearing the lamentation of the grief-afflicted cranes, an old crane said: "Do you act thus; bringing fishes, (and) commencing at the burrow of an ichneumon, spread the fishes along singly in a line as far as the snake's hole; then, by means of that path of food, the snake (will) be perceived by an ichneumon coming along, (and) from his natural enmity (he) will kill (him)." Upon that being done, what has been stated occurred. Now the sound of the young birds up the tree was heard by the ichneumons, (so that) afterwards the young cranes were devoured by that ichneumon. Hence we say, 'Having thought over the remedy,' &c. Seeing you being carried along by us, people will surely say something; hearing that, if you should give a reply, your death will (assuredly) occur; therefore, by all means, stay here." The turtle replied: "(Am) I, then, an idiot? Nothing whatever shall be uttered by me." Then upon that being done, the turtle being carried through the air, all the cow-herds ran after and exclaimed: "Ho! a great marvel! a turtle is being carried by birds!" Then somebody said: "If the turtle falls, then he is to be cooked and eaten here." Another said: "(He is) to be taken home." Someone else said: "Having made him descend, fetching fire and roasting (him), I will eat (him) just here." Hearing this unkind language, forgetting his agreement, he cried out passionately: "You shall eat ashes"; in saying this, he fell from the stick and was killed by the cow-herds. Hence I say, "From well-wishing friends," &c. Now the spy, the crane, coming there said: "Sire! at the very first I indicated, (that) a clearing of the fort should immediately be made; and that was not done by you; hence this has happened (as) the fruit of disregarding that (direction). Sire! This burning of the fort was done by the crow called Cloud-colour, (who was) employed by the vulture." The king, sighing, said:—

11. "He who confides in enemies, either from respect (shown) or assistance (rendered), awakes like one being asleep and fallen from the top of a tree."

Hereupon the spy continued: "After having accomplished the burning of the fort, when this Cloud-colour was come (to him), then Spotted-colour (received him and) graciously said: 'Let this Cloud-colour be inaugurated here in the realm of Camphor-island. For it is thus said:—

12. One should not obliterate the deed of a grateful servant; one should gratify him with a reward, with heart, voice, and look.'"

The ruddy-goose said: "Sire! have (you) heard what the spy says?" The king asked: "What followed?" The spy continued:—Then the chief minister, the vulture said: "Sire! that (is) not proper; let some other favour be conferred. For:—

13. How can there be the displacing of one who is (already) invested with authority? Favour (conferred) on the low, O king! (is) like an impression on the sands.

A low fellow should never be placed in the position of the great. For thus it is said:—

14. A low fellow, having attained a position of dignity, desires to cut off (his) master; as the mouse, having reached the state of a tiger, tried to kill the saint."

Spotted-colour asked, "How (was) that?" The vulture related (as follows):—There was, in the grove of the divine philosopher Gautama, a saint named Great-austerity. In the vicinity of the hermitage a young mouse, (which) had dropped from the mouth of a crow, was found by him; (and) was afterwards nourished with grains of wild rice, by that compassionate saint. By-and-bye, a cat was seen by the saint running after the mouse to eat (it); thereupon, by the power of his devotion, the mouse was transformed into a very strong cat. But the cat, also, (was) timid of a dog; therefore (he) made it a dog; (but) the dog (had) great fear of a tiger; thereupon (he) made it a tiger. Now the saint perceives him, though a tiger, no different from a mouse; hence all the people dwelling there, seeing a tiger, say: "This mouse has been brought to the condition of a tiger by this saint." Hearing this, the tiger uneasily reflected: "As long as this saint shall live, so long the disgraceful story of my origin will not disappear." Having thus reflected he rose up to slay the saint; (but) the saint knowing his design, said "Become a mouse again," (and) immediately made him a mouse. Hence I say, "A low fellow, having attained an exalted station," &c. Furthermore, Sire! this is not to be deemed (so) very easy. Listen:—

15. After devouring many fishes, good, bad, and indifferent, a foolish crane, from excessive gluttony, perished through the grip of a crab.

Spotted-colour asked, how that (was), and (his) minister related (as follows):—There is, in the country of Mâlwa, a lake called Lotus-bearing. There an old crane, who had lost his strength, stood making himself appear as though afflicted; and he was questioned (thus) by a crab from a distance: "How (is it) your Honour is standing here renouncing food?" The crane said: "Listen, good Sir. Fishes (are) the causes of my living; and the fishes here are certainly to be killed by fishermen; this (is) the conversation of the fishermen (which I) heard in the suburbs of the city. Perceiving, therefore, that from the absence of a livelihood from this quarter my death (is) at hand, I have disregarded even food." Then all the fishes reflected, "On the present occasion, at all events, he seems indeed to be our benefactor, therefore let him be asked what is to be done. For thus it is said :—

16. An alliance (may be formed) with an assisting enemy, (but) not with an injuring friend. Helping and injuring is alone worthy to be regarded as the distinguishing characteristic of these two."

The fishes said : "Sir Crane! where (is) the means of our preservation?" The crane said : "There is (as) a means of preservation another lake. I can take you there one by one." The fishes, from fear, said, "Let it be so." Then that wicked crane, taking those fishes one by one into a certain place, (and) having eaten them, returned (and) said : "They have been placed by me in another body of water." Thereupon a crab said to him : "Sir Crane! take me also there." Then the crane, desirous of unprecedented crab's flesh, taking him courteously placed him on the ground. But the crab perceiving fish-bones scattered (over) the surface of the ground, thought: "Alas, unfortunate, I am ruined! Well, now I (must) act suitably to the occasion. For :—

17. As long as a danger (is) not arrived, so long there should be apprehension about (it); perceiving the danger arrived, one should attack it fearlessly.

Besides :—

18. When a wise man attacked perceives nothing advantageous for himself, then he dies fighting with the enemy."

Thinking thus, the crab severed the crane's neck, (and) the crane attained dissolution. Hence I say, "Having eaten many fishes," &c. Then, also, again king Spotted-colour said : "Listen : O prime minister! this is just what I have been thinking of; that, by this Cloud-colour remaining here (as) king, whatever excellent things belong to Camphor island, could be sent (to) us; by that (means) we can remain, with great luxury, in the Vindhya mountains." Far-seeing laughingly said : "Sire !—

19. He who is delighted with a non-realisable speculation, will meet (with) discomfiture, like the Bráhman (who) broke the pots.

The king asked : "How (was) that?" Far-seeing replied :—There was a Bráhman named The-Delight-of-the-Gods, in the city of Goddess-fort. At the (sun's) passing into the equinoctial sign, he received a dish of meal; after having received it, oppressed by the sun he laid down in a potter's shed filled with pots. Then taking a stick in his hand for the protection of the meal, he began to think : If I should sell this dish of meal, I (shall) get ten cowries; then with those cowries, at the present time, having purchased pots, dishes, &c., (and) repeatedly with the increased riches having successively purchased and sold betel-nut, cloth, &c., and having amassed, by trading, riches to the extent of a lakh (of rupees), I (shall) contract four marriages; then, I (shall) bestow most affection upon her who (is) the youngest and most beautiful among them. Thereupon when those wives, become envious, shall be bickering among themselves, then I, irritated with anger, will beat all the women with a stick,"—saying this he thrust forward the stick, smashed the dish of meal, and broke many pots that were in the potter's shed. Then, from hearing the smashing of the pots, the potter, coming, seized (him) by the throat, and turned (him) out of the house. Hence I say, "An unrealisable speculation," &c. Then the king privately asked the vulture (his) minister: "Father! advise me what is to be done." The vulture replied :—

20. "The guides of a king, lifted up with pride like an excited elephant, assuredly incur censure, through his vagaries.

Listen a bit, Sire! Was the fort demolished through our pride of strength, or rather, by an expedient devised by your Majesty's genius?" The king replied: "By an expedient of your Honour." The vulture rejoined: "If my advice be acted on, then let (us) return to our own country ; otherwise, in the rainy season now at hand, on war recommencing with an equal force, a retreat to our own territory will be difficult for us, (who) have lingered in the enemy's country. For the sake of comfort and credit, let (us) make peace (and) retire. The fort (is) dismantled, and the glory acquired. That (is) exactly my opinion. For:—

21. He who, placing duty in front, setting (aside his) master's likes and dislikes, has stated wholesome unpleasantnesses, (is) a (real) assistant (of) the king.

Moreover :—

22. (One) should desire peace with an equal. Victory in war (is) doubtful ; one should not make (it) dubious. Thus said Vrihaspati.

Besides :—

23. Who, not a novice in war, would cause (to be) placed in the swing of uncertainty, an ally, (his) army, (his) kingdom, himself, and reputation?

Besides :—

24. In battle there is sometimes even loss for both (parties). Were not Beauty and Ugliness, equals in heroism, slain the one by the other.

The king said : "How (was) that?" The minister replied :—Formerly two greatly distinguished demons, named Beauty and Ugliness, with intense bodily suffering, for a long time worshipped the Moon-crowned one,* through desiring the sovereignty of the three worlds. At length being satisfied with both of them, the Revered one said: "Ask ye a boon." Immediately, through the dominance of Saraswatî† over these two terrific beings, both, desiring to say one thing, gave utterance to another.—"If your Holiness (is) pleased with us, then let the Supreme Lord give his beloved (wife) Pârvatî." Then the angered Holy One, through the obligation of conferring the boon, and through foolishness, gave Pârvatî. Afterwards, these two world-destroyers,—inflamed by the loveliness of her person, longing in their hearts, darkened by sin, wrangling with each other, saying, " (She is) mine,"—resolved to ask some arbitrator or other. On (this opinion) being formed, even the Lord himself, in the form of an

---

* The god S'iva. † The goddess of speech.

aged Brâhman came and stood (before them). Thereupon they asked the Brâhman: "To which of us two does this one belong: she was obtained by us by our own might?" The Brâhman said:—

25. A Brâhman excellent in wisdom (is) to be honoured; (so is) also a powerful Kshatriya, a Vaiśya, possessed of money and grain; but a Sûdra, through service (done) for the regenerate.

You two, then, (are of) the military profession; fighting (is) truly your allotted duty." On this being said, they both cried out, "Good!" (and) the two equal to one another in strength perished at the same moment by a mutual blow. Hence I say, "One should desire peace with an equal," &c. The king said: "Then why was not this pointed out at the very first?" The minister replied: "Was my advice at that time listened to by Your Majesty to the end? At that time, this war was not commenced with my advice; for this peacefully disposed Gold-egg ought not to be molested. Thus it (is) said:—

26. A truthful (man) one of noble race, a virtuous (man), one of low race, one having many brothers, a strong man, (and) one victorious in many battles,—are renowned (as) the seven (with whom) peace should be made.

27. The truthful cherishes truth; (when) made peace with, he undergoes no change. Even at the risk of life, manifestly, a noble man never approaches ignominy.

28. Truly everyone would fight for a just man (when) attacked. Both from (his) virtue and from the affection of his subjects, a virtuous person (is) hard to be injured.

29. Peace (is) to be made with even the low-born on destruction being imminent; (if) without recourse to that the other cannot gain time.

30. As from its compactness a thick bambu surrounded by thorns cannot be cut asunder; so (neither can he) having many brothers.

31. "The strong should be combatted with,"—there is no such injunction (as this). A cloud never moves against the wind.

32. From the splendour of the son of Jamadagni,* victorious in many battles, everyone is everywhere always subject.

33. (With) whomsoever one victorious in many battles concludes an alliance, his enemies, by the power of that (ally), quickly come into subjection.

Therefore, in the present case, this flamingo, endowed with many (excellent) qualities should be made peace with." The ruddy-goose said: "Spy! (we have) heard all. Go again, (and) having tried him, return quickly." Then gold Gold-egg questioned the ruddy-goose (thus): "Minister! how many should not be made peace with? I wish to know them." The minister replied: "Sire! I (will) relate (them). Listen:—

---

* Paras'u-Râma, fabled to have been many times conqueror of the whole world.

34. A child, an old man, one with a chronic sickness, also one expelled his caste, a coward, one with cowardly people, a covetous person, (and) also one with covetous followers.

35. One whose supporters are disaffected, one greatly attached to sensuality, one, various-minded in counsel, and a dispiser of Gods and Brâhmans.

36. One stricken by fate, one anxious about fate, one afflicted by famine, and one embarrassed by disorganisation of his army.

37. One not dwelling in his country, one with many enemies, one who is not apposite with time, one who swerves from truth and right,—these (are the) twenty men.

38. One should not make peace with these, but should war (with them) merely; these, being warred against, quickly reach subjection (to) the enemy.

39. Mankind is not willing to fight for a child, because of his insignificance; since a boy (is) not able to understand the advantage of fighting and not fighting.

40. An old man, and also one long sick, through want of the power of exertion these two are undoubtedly despised even by themselves.

41. One expelled from all his kindred is easily destroyed; those very relations, gained over, kill him.

42. The coward, through fleeing from battle, destroys himself; so likewise, one with timid troops is deserted by them in battle.

43. The followers of a covetous man do not fight, through the non-division (of the spoil); he is killed by covetous followers (when they are) deprived of gifts.

44. One whose supporters are disaffected is deserted by those supporters in battle; one excessively addicted (to) sensuality is easily overcome.

45. He who is various-minded in counsel is odious (to his) counsellors; from the fickleness of his opinion he is disregarded by them in an emergency.

46. Through the mightiness of religion at all times a despiser of Gods and Brâhmans fades away of himself; so also (does) one stricken by fate.

47. "Fate is veritably the cause of success and of misfortune,"—reflecting thus, the fatalist does not exert himself.

48. One afflicted with famine sinks of himself; there is no strength to fight begotten of one with demoralisation in his army.

49. One not in his own place is destroyed by even an insignificant enemy; an alligator, though very small, in water, drags (in) even an elephant.

50. He who has many enemies (is) scared, like a pigeon among kites; by whatever path he goes, he is beset with danger.

51. He who has arrayed his army unseasonably is slain by one who fights at the (proper) time; as a crow (is killed) by an owl on a starless night.

52. One should never form an alliance with one who swerves from truth and right; although made peace with, from want of probity he soon changes.

I (will) relate yet more. Peace, war, halting, marching, rallying, (and) dividing into two,—(are) the six qualities. The manner of commencing operations, abundance of men and *matériel*, discrimination of place and time, the repulse of assaults, the accomplishment of enterprizes,—(constitute) the five-membered counsel. Conciliation, bribery, dissension, (and) threats,—(are) the four expedients. The power of perseverance, the power of counsel, the power of the king,—(are) the triad of powers. Having attended to all this, they who are desirous of conquest always become great. For:—

53. Fortune which is not to be obtained even at the price of the sacrifice of life, runs incontinently to the house of those skilled in polity.

And thus it is said:—
54. He whose wealth is equitably divided, (whose) spy (is) concealed, (whose) counsel (is) secret, and who speaks not unkindly among (his) fellow-creatures,—he rules the earth bounded by the ocean.

But, Sire! although peace (were) suggested by the prime-minister—the vulture—still (it) would not now be agreed to by that king, through pride of the recent victory. Therefore, let this be done. Let our friend the heron, king of Ceylon, named Great-strength, excite a disturbance in Jambudwîpa. For:—

55. Maintaining great secrecy, an ardent hero, marching about with a very compact force, should inflame the enemy; with whom (when) inflamed (he), equally inflamed, forms an alliance.

The king said: "Let it be so." Having said this he started off the crane named Variegated to Ceylon, giving him a private letter. Now the spy returning said: "Sire! just let the conversation of that (enemy's) place be heard. There the vulture spoke thus,—' Sire! Cloud-colour resided there long; he knows whether king Gold-egg (be) peaceably inclined or not.' Then having called for this Cloud-colour (he) was questioned by Spotted-colour,—'Crow! what kind of king (is) Gold-egg; or the ruddy-goose minister, what (is he) like?' Cloud-colour said: 'Sire! this Gold-egg (is) a king like Yudhishṭhira, magnanimous (and) truthful. A minister like the ruddy-goose is nowhere to be seen.' The king said: 'If so, then how was he deceived by thee?' Cloud-colour laughing said: 'Sire!—

56. What cleverness (is) there in the deception of those inspired with confidence? What, forsooth, (is) the manliness of the slayer of those who, having ascended to the lap, are asleep (there)?

Listen, Sire! I was detected by that minister at the very first glance; but that king (is) magnanimous, therefore (he) was deceived by me. Thus it is said:—

57. He who, by comparison with himself, thinks a rogue (to be) a speaker of the truth, even he is deceived by that (rogue);—as the Brâhman, in respect of the goat.'

The king asked: 'How (was) that?' Cloud-colour related (as follows):—There was, in the province of Gaur, a Brâhman named Worthy-of-sacrifice; and he having gone to another village, and having purchased a white goat, for present sacrifice, placed (it) on (his) shoulder, (and) while hastily going along the road, was seen by three rogues. Then those three rogues, having reflected thus,—" If by any dodge that goat is obtained, then it (will) be a stroke of policy,"—seated (themselves) and remained, in a lonesome spot, under three trees in the path of the Brâhman. Then one rogue addressed the Brâhman: "Sir Brâhman! why art thou carrying a dog on (thy) shoulder?" The Brâhman said: "This (is) not a dog, simpleton! it (is) a goat for sacrifice." Then again the same was said by the second rogue stationed at the distance of a *kos*. Hearing this, the Brâhman said: "This (is) not a dog." Having said which, somewhat disconcerted in mind, (he) placed the goat on the earth, (and) inspecting (it) again and again, replacing (it) on (his) shoulder, he went along wavering in mind. For thus it is said:—

58. Surely the mind of even the good wavers from the speeches of the wicked. He who is induced to trust by them, dies like Wonderful-ear.

The king asked, how that was, (and) he related (the tale as follows):—There was in a part of a certain wood a lion named Arrogant. He (had) three attendants, a crow a tiger, and a jackal. Now, while roaming about, a camel strayed from a caravan was seen by them (and) questioned (thus): "Whence (is) your Honour come?" and he related all the particulars regarding himself. Then, being conducted by them, he was presented to the lion. Then the lion, giving (him) an assurance of protection, (and) conferring the title "Wonderful-ear," retained (him in his service). So the time passes. Now once, through the bodily indisposition of the lion and because of excessive rain, not being able to procure food, they became perplexed. Then the crow, tiger and jackal resolved (thus): "Let (something) be done so that the master kill Wonderful-ear; for what have we (to do) with this corn-eater." The tiger said: "He has been received by the master, (who has) granted (him) an assurance of protection; how, then, is this possible?" Says the crow: "At the present time the weakened master will even commit sin."

For :—
59. Even a woman pinched with hunger will desert (her) child ; a snake pained by hunger will devour its own eggs. What crime will not those suffering hunger commit ? Men wasting away (from famine) become compassion-less.

Besides :—
60. The drunkard, the careless, the frantic, the distressed, the passionate, the famished, the covetous, the coward, the precipitate, and the sensual,—know no law.

Having thus settled (the matter), they all went near to the lion. The lion said : "Has anything been found for food ? " The crow replied : " Sire ! even by (great) exertion nothing has been procured." The lion (then) remarked : " What means of living (is there) now ? " The crow replied : " Through neglecting the food in your power this destruction of all (of us) is imminent." The lion inquired : " What food (is) here in my power ? " The crow whispered in the lion's ear,—" Wonderful-ear ! " The lion having touched the ground, touches both (his) ears (and says) : " I have given him an assurance of safety, therefore, how can such a cruel deed be perpetrated ? Thus—

61. Neither gift of land, nor gift of gold, nor gift of cattle, nor gift of food, (is) as that they here call the greatest gift among all gifts—the gift of security from danger.

Again :—
62. Whatever advantage (arises) from the horse-sacrifice,* fulfilling every desire, that advantage one fully obtains on a fugitive being preserved."

The crow said : " He must not be killed by the master ; but it must be so managed by us that he volunteers the gift of his own body." Hearing that, the lion remained silent. Then he [the crow] finding an opportunity deceitfully took them all, and went towards the lion. Then the crow said : " Sire ! even after (great) effort food has not been obtained, and the master (is) distressed by many fasts. Now, therefore, let my flesh be eaten. For :—

63. Surely all these accessories of royalty are based on the sovereign. Care (bestowed) upon trees with roots, (is) advantageous to men."

The lion replied : " Friend ! better the resignation of life, rather than engaging in such an act as this." The jackal also said the same ; but the lion replied : " Not so." The tiger said : " Let the master subsist by my body." The lion replied : " (That can) never (be) proper." Then, while they were speaking Wonderful-ear also desired to speak ; whereupon the tiger remained in readiness. Then Wonderful-ear also, (his) confidence excited (by) looking at the jackal, crow, and tiger, volunteered his own body. While he was in the act of speaking, the tiger ripping up his flank killed (him), and he was eaten by them all. Hence I say, " Surely the mind wavers," &c. Thereafter, having heard the remark of the third rogue, the Brâhman convinced (that he was) wrong, abandoned the goat, washed (himself), and went home, and the goat was led off and eaten by the rogues. Hence I say, " He who by comparison with himself considers," &c.

---

* One of the most solemn of sacrifices, which won an immensity of merit.

The king said: "Cloud-colour! how (is it) you lived a very long time in the midst of enemies? or how was their conciliation effected?" Cloud-colour replied: "Sire! what is not done by one desirous of the master's interest, or on account of his own purposes. See:—

64. Do not people, O King! carry fuel on their heads to burn? The current of a river, while watering, cuts away the root of a tree.

Thus it is said:—

65. A wise man, having an object (in view) will bear enemies even on his shoulder; as the frogs were destroyed by an old serpent."

The king asked, how that (was); (and) Cloud-colour related (as follows):—There was, in a certain withered garden, a serpent named Slow-crawl; and he, by (reason of) extreme decay (of nature) being unable to seek his own food, laid down on the bank of a pool. Then he was seen and questioned from a distance by a certain frog. "Why are you not searching (for) food?" The serpent replied: "Friend! go. What (advantage will accrue to) thee by inquiring into the circumstances of helpless me?" Then the frog, (his) curiosity being aroused, said to the serpent: "By all means let it be related." The serpent replied: "Friend! here in Brahmapura, the son of the Brâhman named Kauṇḍinya, about twenty years old, endowed with every virtue, was, by ill-luck, maliciously bitten by me. Then seeing his son named Well-disposed lying dead, Kauṇḍinya, become insensible through grief, rolled upon the earth. Thereupon all his kinsmen, the inhabitants of Brahmapura, came there, (and) sat down. Thus it is said:—

66. He is a relative who stands (by one) in a challenge (to combat), in adversity, in a famine, in a contest with the enemy, at the king's gate, and in the cemetery.

Then a householder Brâhman named Kapila spoke: "O Kauṇḍinya! thou art a fool, because thou complainest thus. Listen:—

67. As transitoriness from the very first takes to its bosom, like a nurse, the one (just) born, (and) afterwards the (true) mother (does so),—then what way for grief (is there)?

In like manner:—

68. Whither are gone the rulers of the earth, with their guards, armies, and chariots? The earth remains even now a witness of their departure.

Again:—

69. This body is not perceived (to be) every moment wasting away. Like an unbaked pot standing in water, (when) dissolved (the fact) is discovered.

70. Day by day Death approaches nearer the vicinity of a living creature; just as slaughter (to) a victim being led along step by step.

For:—

71. Transitory (is) youth, beauty, life, a store of goods, lordly dignity, (and) the society of a loved one. A wise man is not fascinated (by these).

72. As one piece of wood and another piece of wood may meet together in the ocean; and, having met, may part (again),—such-like (is) the meeting of human beings.

73. As any traveller, having taken refuge, rests in the shade, and having refreshed (himself) again goes (onwards) ;—such-like (is) the meeting of human beings.

Again :—

74. What lamentation (need there be) over a body constructed with five (elements), resuming the quintuple character, each element finding again its own birth-place?"

75. As many connections, dear to the soul, as a living creature forms, so many thorns of grief are they [the connections] planting in his heart.

76. This (is) not a permanent dwelling (which) is gained by anyone, even with his own body; how much less with anyone else!

Moreover :—

77. Union, indeed, proves the possibility of separation; just as birth (does) the approach of inevitable death.

78. Truly the end of unions with beloved (objects), delightful for the present moment,—is distressing; like (that of) unwholesome foods.

Again :—

79. As the streams of rivers flow on, (and) return not; so also day and night for ever (proceed), taking (with them) the life of mortals.

80. The society of the good, which (is) the flavour of happiness in the world, is yoked to the carriage-pole of miseries, from its ending in separation.

81. For this very reason the virtuous do not desire the society of the good; for, there is no medicine for a heart cut by the sword of separation.

82. Although deeds have been well done by kings Sagara* and the rest, still those very deeds, and they also, have gone to destruction.

83. (By) meditating and meditating over that inexorable punisher Death, all the efforts of even a clever man become relaxed; like a leathern thong soaked by rain-water.

84. The very first night (on) which the strongest of human beings attains abidance in the womb, thenceforward, with unfaltering march, he proceeds day by day towards Death.

Then reflect (on) the world. This grief (is) an evolution of ignorance. Observe :—

85. Ignorance would not be the cause, if separation (were) the cause; then let grief increase as the time passes away. What removes (grief)?

Therefore, friend! compose yourself. Dismiss all talk of sorrow. For :—
86. For the blows of deep grief produced not by the fall of arrows (but) by vital-

---

* An ancient king, fabled to have conquered many nations; and to perform the funeral ceremonies of whose sixty thousand sons, the river Ganges was brought down from heaven.

piercing weapons, the greatest medicine (is) not to think (about them)."

Then having heard his speech, as though awakened, Kauṇḍinya sat up (and) said: "Enough now (of) this dwelling in the house of hell! I (will) go to the forest."

Kapila continued:—

87. "Even in a wood evils prevail over the sensual; while in a house the restraint of the five senses (is) a penance. The home of one free from passions engaged in a worthy act (is) a grove of penance.

For:—

88. Although afflicted one should practise virtue, in whatever station of life engaged, evenly among all creatures. The badge (is) not the cause of virtue.*

And it has been said:—

89. They surmount difficulties whose eating (is merely) for sustenance, (whose) sexual intercourse (is) for offspring, and (whose) speech (is) for the utterance of truth.

Again:—

90. The soul (is) a river, (whose) holy confluence is self-restraint, (whose) water (is) truth, (whose) bank (is) morality, (whose) waves (are) compassion. Here perform ablutions, O son of Pâṇḍu! The inward soul is not purified by water.

And especially:—

91. (There is) happiness for one quitting this excessively sapless world, attacked with the pains of birth, death, decay, and disease.

92. Pain actually exists; happiness (does) not†;—that is evident, because, in the alleviation of those distressed with pain, the word ' happiness' is employed."

Kauṇḍinya said: "(It is) even so." After that, I was cursed by that disconsolate Brâhman, thus,—"Beginning from this day, thou shalt be a carrier of frogs."

Kapila added: "At the present time thou (art) unable to bear admonition; thy heart (is) full of grief; nevertheless hear what ought to be done,—

93. Society should be shunned with all the soul; but if it cannot be relinquished, it should be formed with the good. The very society of the good (is healing) medicine.

Again:—

94. Passion should be relinquished with all the soul; but if it cannot be relinquished, it should be indulged towards one's own wife: she (is) indeed the (proper) remedy for that."

Hearing that, Kauṇḍinya, the fire of (whose) grief (was) extinguished by the nectar of the advice of Kapila, took the (pilgrim's) staff, according to the (sacred) precepts. Since then, I remain here to experience the Brâhman's curse (and) to carry frogs. Thereupon, that frog going reported all (to) Web-foot, the chief of the frogs. Then the chief of the frogs coming, leaping with joy, placed himself upon the serpent's back. The serpent, taking him on (his) back, wandered off at a brisk pace. The next day the chief of the frogs said to him (as he was) unable to move: "Why (are) you to-day (so) sluggish?" The serpent replied: "Sire! from want of food I am weak." The frog-chief (then) said: "By my command eat the frogs." Then having replied, "This great favour (is) accepted (thankfully)," gradually the serpent

---

* It is not the cowl that makes the monk.
† That is, pain is positive; happiness is negative.

devoured the frogs; then seeing the pool denuded of frogs, he devoured the frog-chief also. Hence I say, "One should bear the enemy on the shoulder even," &c. Sire! now let the relation of tales of former events cease. This king Gold-egg (is) on every account to be conciliated, let him be made peace with; that (is) my opinion." The king replied: "What an idea (is) this of yours! Since he has been thus conquered by us, therefore if, by my command, he live in servitude, let it be so; otherwise, let him be (further) attacked." Hereupon, the parrot coming from Jambudwîpa said: "Sire! a heron, the king of Ceylon, overrunning Jambudwîpa now occupies (it)." The king hastily said to him: "What? what?" The parrot repeated (what he had) said before. The vulture said within himself: "Well done! O great minister ruddy-goose! well done!" The king angrily exclaimed: "Let him stay until I go (and) tear him up by the roots." Far-seeing smiling said :—

95. "A roaring noise, like (that of) an autumn cloud, should not uselessly be made. A great man never proclaims the gain or disadvantage of the enemy.

Moreover :—

96. A king should not make war upon many opponents at once. Even a fierce serpent (is) infallibly destroyed by swarming insects.

Sire! is there to be a march hence without a peace? In that case, a commotion would be raised in our rear by him. Besides :—

97. The fool who, without knowing the gist of the matter, becomes subject to anger, is afflicted in the same manner as the Brâhman on account of the ichneumon."

The king asked: "How (was) that?" Far-seeing related (as follows) :—There was in Ujjayin a Brâhman named Honey. His wife had been confined, and she, leaving her husband for the protection of her young offspring, went to perform ablutions. Now a man was sent by the king to fetch that Brâhman for the performance of a Pûrvana-śrâddha.* Perceiving him, the Brâhman, through his natural poverty, reflected, "If I do not go quickly, somebody else will get the fee. It is said :—

98. The time in which it is not being done quickly drinks up the spirit of (any) act which is to be accepted, given, or done.

And there is nobody (to act as) protector of the child, therefore what am I to do? Well! leaving for the protection of the child this ichneumon, (which) for a long time has been cherished in no wise different from (my own) child, I (will) go." This (he) did, (and) went. Afterwards, a black snake silently approaching near the child was killed and rent in pieces by the ichneumon. Then the ichneumon perceiving the Brâhman returning, with feet and mouth smeared with blood, hastily approaching rolled at the Brâhman's feet. Then the Brâhman, seeing him in that condition, thinking that his son had been eaten by him, killed him with his staff. Immediately thereafter, as soon as he approached (and) looked, perceiving the child sweetly sleeping and the dead snake close by it, he experienced the deepest anguish. Hence I say, "Without knowing the gist of the matter," &c.

---

* An offering to ancestors at the changes of the moon.

Moreover:—

99. Lust, anger, covetousness, envy, pride, rashness,—this six-fold class one should forsake; on its being forsaken, one may be happy.

The king said: "Minister! this (is) thy conviction." The minister replied: "Even so. For:—

100. Recollection in important matters, deliberation, accuracy of knowledge, firmness, secrecy in counsel, (is) the first quality of a minister.

And it is said:—

101. One should not perform an act rashly; inconsiderateness is the source of the greatest misfortunes. Successes, covetous of merit, spontaneously seek him who acts with deliberation.

Therefore, Sire! if my advice is acted on, then, make peace (and) depart. For:—

102. Although four expedients are pointed out in the accomplishment of peace, (this is) a mere enumeration. The upshot of them (is) a success based on negociation."

The king said: "How is that to be speedily effected?" The minister replied: "Sire! it will soon be (effected). For:—

103. A wicked person is like an earthen pot, easy to break and hard to join together again; but a good person, like a vessel of gold, (is) hard to sever, but quickly to be united.

Besides:—

104. An ignorant man (is) easily to be conciliated, a well-informed man is conciliated more easily; but not even Brahmâ conciliates a man puffed up with a smattering of knowledge.

And especially (bear in mind),—that king knows his duty, and the minister knows everything. This was perceived by me formerly from the remarks of Cloud-colour, and from perceiving the acts performed by him. For:—

105. The natures of qualities out of sight should everywhere be judged by acts; therefore, by results one should estimate the conduct of those acting out of sight."

The king said: "Enough (of) debating; let it be done as desired." Having given this advice, the prime-minister—the vulture—went into the fort saying, "What is proper (is) to be done there." Thereupon the crane (who was) the spy, came (and) informed king Gold-egg: "Sire! the prime-minister—the vulture—has approached us to make peace." The flamingo said: "Minister! some designing (person) must be again coming here." The minister smiling said: "Sire! this is no cause of alarm; for this Far-seeing (is) a gentleman. But this (is) the habit of the dull-witted,—sometimes no suspicion towards an enemy is entertained; at other times suspicion (is) everywhere. Just as—

106. A wary goose seeking the young shoots of the lotus in the night, on a lake with manifold reflections of stars, was momentarily deceived; again, even in the day-time he (will) not nibble the white lotus, suspecting (it to be) a star. A person (once) alarmed by deception anticipates disaster even in truth itself.

SANDHI.

107. For a mind spoiled by the wicked there is no confidence even in the good. Does not a child scalded by porridge eat even curds (after they have been) blow upon.

Therefore, Sire! according to your ability, let (some) article (such as) a complimentary present of jewels and the like, be made ready to do him honour." On this being done accordingly, the vulture—the minister—being courteously led from the gate of the fort by the ruddy-goose, was introduced to the king, and seated in a place provided for him. The ruddy-goose said: "Great minister! all (is) subject to your Honour; let this realm be enjoyed according to your pleasure." The flamingo said: "Even so." Far-seeing replied: "This (is) indeed so; but now a multiplicity of words (is) needless. For:—

108. The covetous should be won over with money; the haughty, by joining the hands.* A fool, by humouring his inclination; a wise man, with truth.

Again :—
109. One should win a friend by good nature, a relative, by courtesy; women and servants, by gifts and honours; other people, by dexterity.

Therefore, now having made peace, let (us) be gone. King Spotted-colour (is) very powerful." The ruddy-goose said: "Let it be declared how peace is to be made." The flamingo added: "How many kinds of peace are possible?" The vulture replied: "I (will) relate (them). Listen :—

110. A king attacked by a stronger, (being) in difficulty, having no other help, should desire peace, causing procrastination.

111. Kapâla, Upahâra, Santâna, Sangata, Upanyâsa, Pratîkâra, Sanyoga, Purushântara,

112. Adrishtanara, Âdishta, Âtmâdishta, Upagraha, Parikraya, Uchchhinna, Parabhûshana.

113. And the Skandhopaneya peace ;—these sixteen are well known. Thus, they who are discriminative in alliances declare peace to be sixteen-fold.

114. The Kapâla-peace (is) to be understood (as) simply an equal peace ;† that which results from a gift is called Upahâra.

115. The Santâna-peace (is) to be understood (as) preceded by the gift of a daughter; alliance with the good, in a friendly manner, (is) called Sangata.

116. The duration (of the last is) as long as life, depending on equal interests ; it is broken by no causes either in prosperity or in adversity.

117. This same Sangata-peace, from its excellence, (is) like gold ; thus it is called

---

* A token of respect.
† A peace made on equal terms. *Kapâla* = a skull, and a water-pot ; both sides of which are exactly alike.

Kánchana* by others skilled in alliances.

118. The (peace) which is effected for the accomplishment of the mere purposes of profit has been called Upanyâsa † by those skilled in (profitable) investments.

119. The peace which is formed on this principle—"Formerly a service was done for him by me; he will do the same for me," is called Pratîkâra.‡

120. "I am helping him, he will also help me,"—this also (is) Pratîkâra; like (that) of Râma and Sugrîva.§

121. Where the well-united authorities go to work wholly for one object, that is called a Sanyoga (peace).‖

122. "Let our purpose be effected by the chief warriors of us two;"—the peace in which (this) stipulation is made (is) the Purushântara.¶

123. "By thee alone is this my purpose to be accomplished";—where the enemy should make this promise, that (is) known (as) the Adrishṭapurusha.**

124. Where he is quit of the enemy by ceding a portion of territory, (and) peace is made,—that is called Âdishṭa†† by those acquainted with alliances.

125. A peace effected by one's own army, is called Âtmâdishṭa‡‡ (that which) is made for the preservation of life, after giving up everything, (is) the Upagraha.§§

126. (The peace which is effected) by part of the treasure, by half the treasure, or even by all the treasure, for the purpose of saving what is left, (is) called Parikraya.‖‖

127. (The peace resulting) from a cession of the most fertile lands is called Uchchhinna; ¶¶ (that) by the giving up of all the fruits raised upon a territory (is) the Parabhûshaṇa *** (peace).

128. Where the fruit reaped is presented on every shoulder, that peace is called by those discriminative in alliances Skhandhopaneya.†††

129. Four alliances are, also, to be discriminated,—mutual assistance, friendship, relationship, and Upahâra.‡‡‡

130. The peace Upahâra is the only one approved by me; apart from Upahâra all (are) deprived of friendship.

131. From his greater strength the enemy does not retire without having gained (something); therefore, except the Upahâra, no other peace exists (for him).

---

* Golden.   † Deposit or investment.   ‡ Requital.
§ Sugrîva was the monkey-king, who with his army of monkeys assisted Râma to conquer Râvaṇa and win back Sîta.   ‖ Union.   ¶ The peace of "another person."
** "The disregarded person"; because the rights of one party are entirely ignored.
†† Assigned.   ‡‡ Assigned by self.   §§ Grasping.
‖‖ Buying off.   ¶¶ Cut off.
*** "Adorning another." Prof. M. Müller prefers paribhûshaṇa, "fully adorning," because it is so given in the Kâmandakîya Nîtisâra.   ††† Shoulder-borne.   ‡‡‡ A complimentary present.

The king said: "Your Honours (are) great scholars, therefore, in the present case, let what should be done (by) us be pointed out." Far-seeing replied: "Ah! what is said?—

132. Who, indeed, would act inconsistently with justice for the (sake of the) body, (which) to-day or to-morrow (is doomed) to destruction by the pains of mental and bodily anguish?

133. Truly the life of corporeal beings (is like) the trembling of the moon in water: knowing it to be of that character one should ever practise virtue.

134. Perceiving the transitory world (to be) like a mirage, one should associate with the good, for (the sake of) virtue, and for (the sake of) happiness.

Therefore, with my concurrence, let the same be done.

135. (If) a thousand horse-sacrifices and truth were weighed by a balance, truth would certainly be more weighty than a thousand horse-sacrifices.

Therefore, let the peace called 'Golden,' be concluded between these two monarchs, preceded by the oath called Truth." Know-all said: "Let it be so." Then the minister Far-seeing was honoured with complimentary presents of robes, &c. Thereupon, pleased, (and) contented at heart, Far-seeing, taking the ruddy-goose (with him), went towards the peacock king. There king Spotted-colour, at the suggestion of the vulture, conversed with Know-all, (having) previously (conferred upon him) honours and gifts. Having agreed to a peace of the kind (above specified, Know-all) was sent back to the flamingo. Far-seeing (then) said: "Sire! what we desired (is) accomplished; now let us return to our own place, the Vindhya mountain." Then having returned to their own place, they enjoyed the result desired by their hearts.

Vishṇuśarman said: "What more (can) I tell, declare it." The princes replied: " Sir, by your Honour's favour every branch of royal procedure has been learnt; therefore, we are delighted." Vishṇuśarman said: "Although (that is) so, still let this all be added :—

136. Let peace (and) happiness always be (the portion) of all victorious monarchs! May the good be free from misfortune! May the fame of those who perform good deeds long increase! May polity, like a loved mistress (be) ever on the breast of kings, (and) kiss the lips of ministers! May there be daily a great festival!"

Here ends the fourth chapter of the Hitopadeśa, called Peace.

FINIS.

ERRATA.

TEXT.

Line.				
386.	For	चेचमस्ति	read	चेचमस्ति
527.	,,	मसीपं	,,	समीपं
818.	,,	त जन्नुः	,,	ते जन्नुः
850.	,,	सर्वेर्वेनवाषिमिः	,,	सर्वेर्वेनवाषिभिः
964.	,,	तयः	,,	यतः
1212.	,,	दत्यादि	,,	दत्यादि
1342.	,,	दुनी	,,	दूनी
1369.	,,	कार्येषु	,,	कार्येषु
1682.	,,	निरस्क्रियते	,,	निरस्क्रियते
2081.	,,	तच सर्वं	,,	तच सर्वं-
2101.	,,	सत्याचवर्षी	,,	षपाचवर्षी
2432.	,,	रक्षत्	,,	रक्षेत्
2639.	,,	प्रयत्नाः	,,	प्रयत्नाः
2640.	,,	नरलोकधीरः	,,	नरलोकवीरः

VOCABULARY.

p. 121, col. 1, line 15. *For* चनहुहुवते *read* चनुहुते
p. 168, col. 1, line 27. ,, चेतक ,, चेटक and transpose the entry.

London: Printed by W. H. Allen & Co., 13 Waterloo Place.

www.ingramcontent.com/pod-product-compliance
Lightning Source LLC
Chambersburg PA
CBHW020154170426
43199CB00010B/1029